Time
Money
Measurement

a Forget Memorization book

Easy learning through images, stories, hands-on activities, & patterns

by Sarah K Major

child1st.com

Right-Brained Time, Money, Measurement

ISBN: 978-1-947484-00-9

Printed in the United States of America

To request more information regarding the copyright policy, contact:

Child1st Publications
PO Box 150226
Grand Rapids, MI 49515
800-881-0912

info@child1st.com

For other teaching and learning resources designed for visual, tactile, kinesthetic and other right-brained learners, visit www.child1st.com.

Other books and materials by this author:

Alphabet Tales
The Illustrated Book of Sounds & Their Spelling Patterns
The Easy-for-Me™ Children's Readers
The Easy-for-Me™ Reading Program
Right-Brained Math Series
SnapWords® sight words
SnapWords® Complete Spelling Dictionary

ABOUT THIS BOOK

This book is for children who are strongly visual, who learn all at once through pictures, are drawn to patterns, rely on body motions, and who need to understand the process behind each math problem they solve. Child1st teaching and learning resources all follow the principle of conveying learning pieces using a variety of right-brain-friendly elements. We take learning tidbits that utilize symbols (numbers and letters) and abstractions, which are left-brained, and embed them in right-brained elements to beautifully integrate the left and right hemispheres in the brain.

RIGHT-BRAINED ELEMENTS:

1- We embed symbols in *VISUALS* so that the child can take a quick look, absorb the learning piece, and store it as an image to be retrieved intact later.

2- We use *PERSONIFICATION* which is a powerful element in teaching and learning. The use of personification makes for rapid learning because the very look and personality of the character conveys the substance of the learning. For example, Ollie Owl, Molly Mongoose, and Sammy Stork have personalities that help cement their function in children's memory. Ollie Hour is an owl who marks the hours and goes very slowly on his short legs. Molly Minute is a mongoose who ticks off the minutes, scuttling around the clock quickly. Sammy Second is a stork who swoops around the clock marking off the seconds.

3- We rely on *PATTERN DISCOVERY* as a way of making numbers come alive and as a means of conveying the amazing relationships between numbers. What results is number sense. Because the brain is a pattern seeking organ, it is drawn to material that follows patterns.

4- We use *STORY* to contain the meaning of what we are teaching in math. Stories, like visuals, make learning unforgettable. They explain the "why" behind math concepts and tie everything together, creating a vehicle for meaning and for recall.

5- We use *BODY MOTION*—both gesture and whole body movement that mirrors the symbol shape or the action in the math story (such as addition or subtraction). Again, body movement is a powerful agent for learning and remembering. For many people, body motion makes recall effortless if the learning piece is directly tied to a unique motion.

6- We employ *VISUALIZATION*—a powerful tool for right-brain-dominant learners. If these learners are given time to transfer the image on the paper in front of them to their brains (prompt them to close their eyes and SEE it in their mind's eye), they will be able to retrieve that image later. If the image contains learning concepts, this is how they will remember what you want them to learn. So in this book, each time a visual is introduced, prompt the student(s) to "see" the image in their mind.

HOW TO USE THIS BOOK

You may approach this book in several ways, depending upon your particular needs, the level and ages of the children you are teaching, and your time constraints. There are three sections for Time, Money, and Measurement. The material presented in each section begins at the very beginning and increases in difficulty. Simply go as far as your student(s) can go in each section.

TABLE OF CONTENTS

Part I - Time

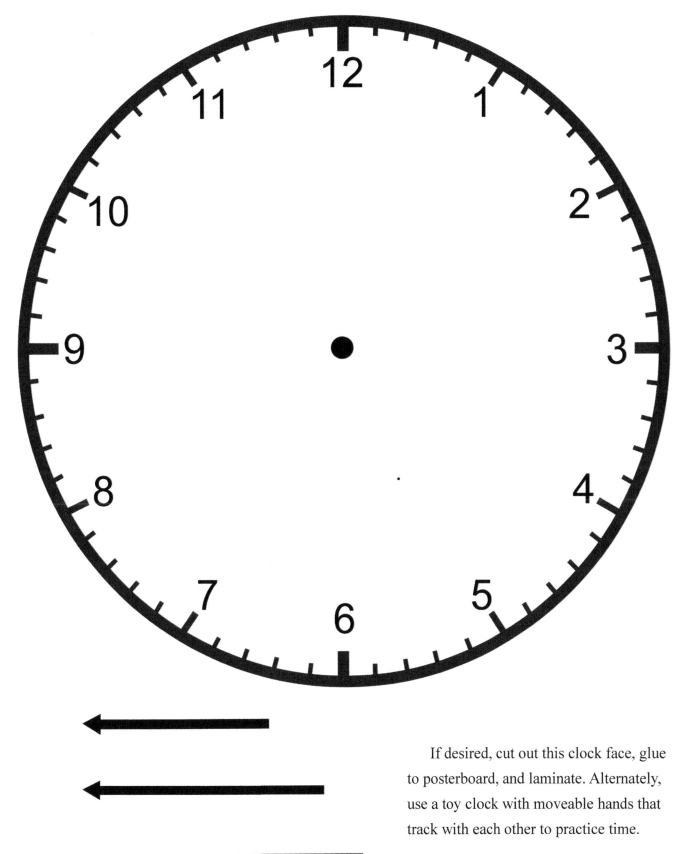

If desired, cut out this clock face, glue to posterboard, and laminate. Alternately, use a toy clock with moveable hands that track with each other to practice time.

This page purposely left blank.

1 Meet Ollie Hour

The three friends couldn't be more different!

Telling time will be taught using stories, visuals, and hands-on activities to make learning and remembering a cinch for the child. There are three main characters in our story about time: Ollie Hour, Molly Minute, and Sammy Second. Ollie is an owl who waddles around the clock face on his short legs, Molly is a mongoose who runs around quickly, and Sammy is a stork with very long legs who runs around fastest of all. We are going to get to know each character one at a time, beginning with Ollie Hour.

A. Ollie Hour counts hours

Ollie Hour starts marking the hours by pointing straight up to the 12 [Figure 1-2, pg. 8]. At the starting gun, he begins to waddle towards the 1. It takes Ollie a whole hour to reach 1, but Ollie is patient and keeps on waddling away without stopping. When he finally reaches the 1, we say, "It is 1 o'clock." [Figure 1-3] When Ollie gets to 2, we say, "It is 2 o'clock." [Figure 1-4] When he reaches 3, we say, "It is 3 o'clock" and so on.

RULE: When we say the time, we say Ollie's number first, then we say "o'clock."

Here are some pictures of Ollie on different hours. The first clock face that is round is an analog clock (it's round like a log) with hands to mark the time. The second clock is a digital clock that has numbers and no hands. Ollie's time goes in the space on the left. These clocks both say "12 o'clock."

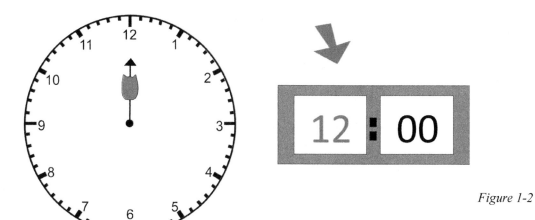

Figure 1-2

These clocks both say "1 o'clock."

Figure 1-3

These clocks both say "2 o'clock."

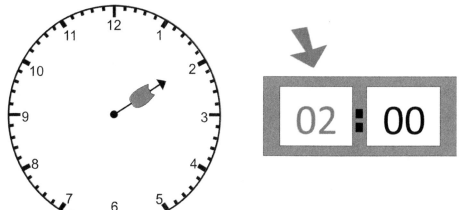

Figure 1-4

 Use resource 1-1 to give your child practice writing hours on analog and digital clocks. Also, use a toy clock and have your child move the hour hand to the times you say.

B. What do a.m. and p.m. mean?

Morning stretches from 12 midnight to 12 noon. When we are telling time, we call morning "a.m.," which stands for "ante meridiem." Ante Meridiem is Latin for "before midday." "Ante" means before, "meri" means "middle" and "diem" means "day." When we are telling time, we call afternoon and evening "p.m.." "P.m." stands for "post meridiem." Post Meridiem is Latin for "after midday."

There are several words in our language that start with "ante" or "before."
- "Anteroom" is a room you pass through before entering a main room. An example of an anteroom is a
- waiting room in a doctor's office.
- "Antenatal" means "before birth." Often mothers have antenatal classes - classes they take before the baby
- is born.
- "Antepast" is food you eat before you eat the regular meal.

Words that begin with "post" include "postdate" (date it after today), "postpone" (put it off until later), and "post operative" (it happens after the operation).

Ollie left at 12 midnight (or midway through the night). As Ollie waddled away from the 12, it was the very earliest part of the morning. Follow Ollie's progress on the picture below.

At midday, as soon as Ollie leaves the 12 again, it is afternoon and we say p.m. This time stretches from 12 noon to 12 midnight.

On the left is a picture that shows a.m. on the left and p.m. on the right, midday at the top, and midnight at the bottom.

It takes Ollie 12 hours to waddle from 12 midday to 12 midnight! Then 12 more hours to go from 12 midnight to 12 midday.

If Ollie is walking after midnight, he will say, "It is 7 a.m.," for example. If he is walking after 12 midday, he will say, "It is 4 p.m."

It makes a big difference when we are telling time to use the a.m. or p.m.! If I ask my friend what time she has breakfast, she would say 7 a.m. because 7 p.m. is closer to when she would go to bed!

 Use resource 1-2 to give your child practice with using a.m. or p.m. Your child will answer questions about what time he or she does certain things and the answers will include a.m. or p.m.

RULE: When we speak of morning hours, we say a.m. When we speak of afternoon and evening hours, we say p.m.

Meet Molly Minute

So far, so good! But wait! What if your activities don't happen right on the hour? What if you get up at 6:15 instead of 6:00? Or what if you eat breakfast at 7:45 instead of at 7:00? This is where knowing Molly Minute is super important!

Molly Minute is a mongoose with legs quite a bit longer than Ollie's. A mongoose is able to hustle pretty fast, and Molly certainly does hustle! She is able to completely circle the clock in the time it takes Ollie to waddle from one number to the next!

But let's back up a minute. Whenever Ollie is pointing to a number and we are saying "o'clock," Molly is always pointing straight up to the 12, the starting point. Here are some examples of what "o'clock" looks like when Molly is in the race with Ollie:

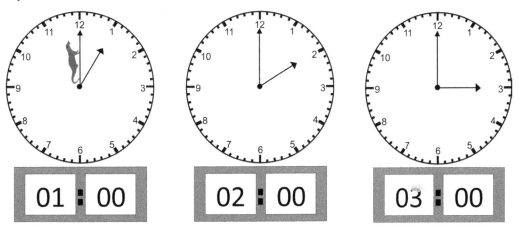

Use resource 2-1 to give your child practice drawing both minute and hour hands to show the hour. You may also practice with toy clocks with hands that track with each other. In each case, the minute hand will be straight up marking the hour with Ollie.

Notice the little lines on the clock between Ollie's numbers. These are Molly's minutes. She doesn't have numbers, but that doesn't bother her at all! She knows that every time she reaches one of Ollie's numbers, she will have marked 5 minutes! Let's say Ollie is on 7 o'clock. He is pointing to the 7 and Molly is pointing straight up to the 12. This is what the clock looks like:

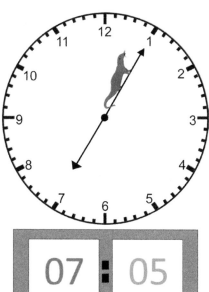

On the digital clock, Ollie's 7 is in the left window. Molly's minutes will be put in the right window. The reason she only has zeros at this point is that she has not started to race yet. When she is pointing straight up, she is at the starting point, but has not begun to run.

BANG! The starting gun goes off! You can barely see Ollie Hour moving, but Molly Minute is ticking off her minutes - 1, 2, 3, 4, 5! Now the clocks look different. Molly is pointing to the 1 and Ollie is pretty much still near the 7 also!

Even though Molly is pointing to the 1, notice that the digital clock on the left shows her minutes at 5. This is right! Molly has traveled 5 minutes since she left the 12.

When Molly races, you can count by 5's. Each time she comes to another one of Ollie's hours, you would say the next 5. Below is what a clock would look like with both Ollie's hours and Molly's minutes.

Molly's minutes are orange. When she is on the 12 before the race starts, she has 00 minutes. When she reaches Ollie's 1, she has run 5 minutes. When she reaches Ollie's 2, she will have run 10 minutes.

On this clock, we say the time like this: "It is 7:05." We say Ollie's hour first, and then we say Molly's minutes.

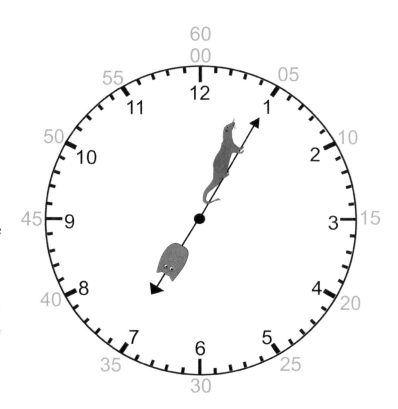

Molly is amazing! In the time it takes Ollie to waddle from the 7 to the 8, Molly will have circled the whole clock face one time - from 12 back around to 12 again.

Let's practice telling time as Ollie and Molly race. Here are three clocks showing how the race is going. Practice reading the time. Look at the black hour numbers first, then add the orange number Molly is pointing to.

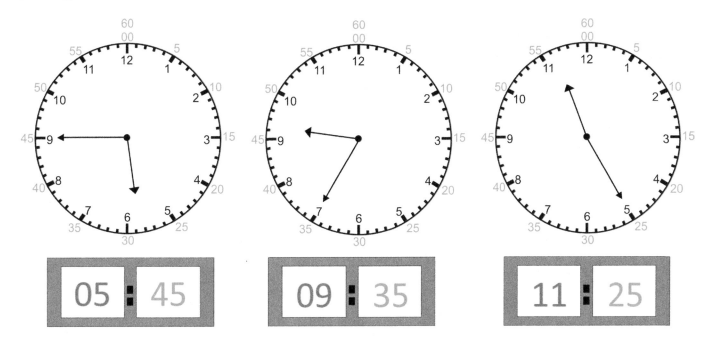

Notice in the three clocks above that Ollie is not pointing exactly to the hour. He has passed the hour a bit while Molly was racing around marking her minutes. When you are telling time, pay attention to the hour Ollie has already passed because he won't always be right on the number. Ollie doesn't mark the new hour until he actually passes it.

In the first clock, Molly has already traveled 45 minutes, so Ollie is almost to the 6! In the second clock, Ollie has passed the 9 and is moving towards the 10. Same goes for the last clock that shows Ollie having passed 11.

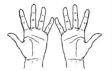

Give your child a toy clock. Call out times and have him/her first set Ollie's hour, then set Molly's minute hand on the correct numbers.

RULE: When we tell time, we say the hour Ollie is on or has just passed. Next we say Molly's minutes.

Finding Patterns in Minutes

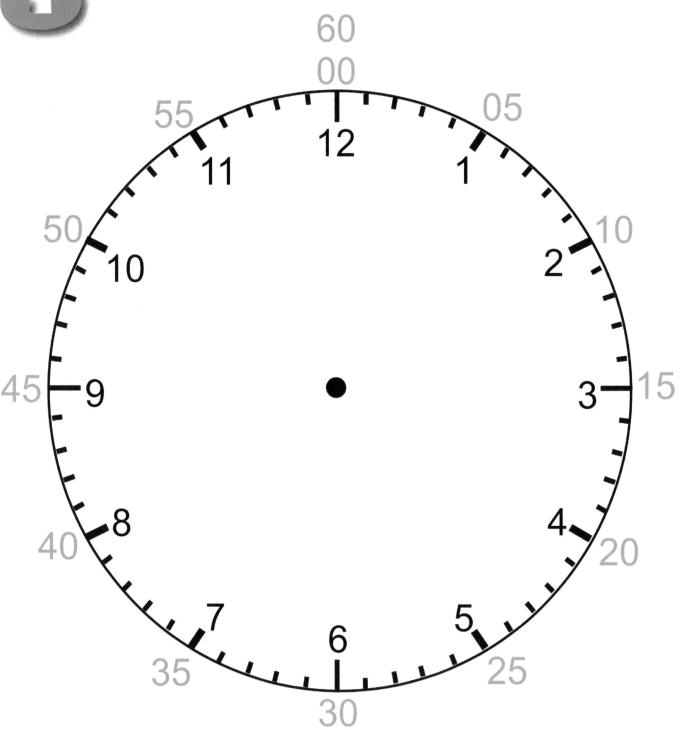

It helps make telling time easy when we are very familiar with Molly's minutes. In this lesson we will spend some time looking for patterns in the numbers and also doing some arm movements to help us relate numbers to each other. Let's look for patterns first.

In the first clock, we are looking at the 1's place in each number. The circled numbers are all zeros. Notice that every other number ends in a zero, starting with the 00//60 at the top of the clock. Six numbers in all end in a zero. The numbers in between all end in a 5. The pattern here is 0, 5, 0, 5 etc.

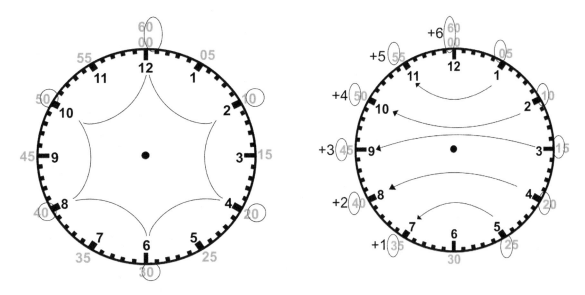

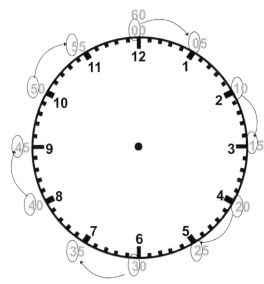

In the second clock above, we are looking in the 10's place. Start by looking at the bottom number: 30. Now look at the numbers on either side of the 30: 25 and 35. When we go from 25-35, the 10's place gets 1 bigger. Now, look at the next two numbers: 20 and 40. Notice that the 10's place is 2 bigger.

In the next pair of numbers, the 10's place gets 3 bigger, then 4 bigger in the next pair of numbers. Finally in 05 and 55, the 10's place gets 5 bigger.

At the top of the clock, the 10's place is 6 bigger. The pattern in the pairs of 10's is +1, +2, +3, +4, etc.

The third clock (above) shows the patterns in the 10's place as you start at noon and circle the clock. There is 0, 0, 1, 1, 2, 2, 3, 3, 4, 4, 5, 5, and finally a 6.

Let's get our whole bodies involved this time. Start by having your child stand up straight with arms down to his/her sides. Let your child see the big clock on page 14 as he mimics the positions of the pairs of numbers with his/her arms.

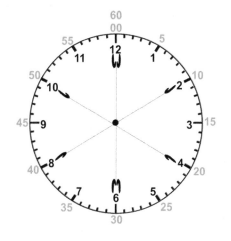

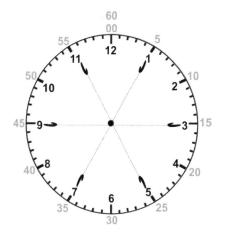

Say, "When I say '30,' both arms point straight down."

Say, "When I say '60,' both arms point straight up."

Say, "When I say '15 and 45,' point your arms straight out to your sides like wings."

Say, "When I say '05 and 55,' point your arms up close to the top of the clock."

Say, "When I say '25 and 35,' point your arms down low, close to the bottom of the clock."

Say, "When I say '10 and 50,' point your arms out above center."

Say, "When I say '20 and 40,' point your arms out, just below center."

Practice like this, mixing it up, until your child is very familiar with the positions of the various minutes. After you have practiced the body version of Molly's minutes, give your child a pointer of some kind and have him/her be Ollie and Molly.

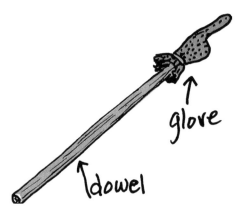

glove

dowel

Use an old shower curtain or an old bedsheet on which you have drawn a circle and the numbers for the clock face. Call out a time and have your child show the hour with his/her arm and show the minutes with the pointer.

You can make a great and fun pointer. Finally, the picture on the right shows a child preparing to listen to you give a time. He will use his fabulous pointer to mark the minutes, and his left arm to mark the hours.

What a child feels in his/her body is stored in memory so that learning becomes permanent.
Here are some times you can call out: 4:30, 7:15, 2:45, 1:10, 12:40, 11:50, 6:20, 5:35, 8:05, 3:25, 9:55, 10:00

Meet Sammy Second

Now that you know all about Molly Minute, Sammy Second will be a piece of cake! Sammy acts just like Molly, except that he is much faster! In the time it takes Molly to get from one little mark to the next, Sammy can circle the whole clock!

Sammy is the red hand with no arrowhead. Look at the clocks below for some examples of telling time with Ollie, Molly, and Sammy. Sammy's seconds go in the third box.

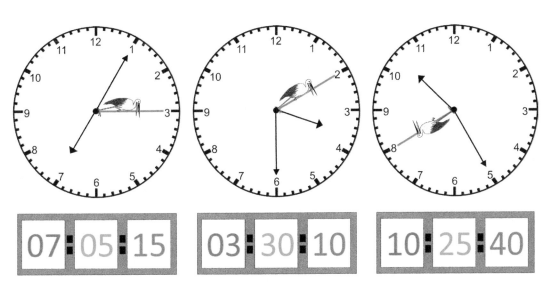

The first clock shows the time to be 7 hours, 05 minutes, and 15 seconds. We would say "Seven oh five and fifteen seconds." The second clock shows 3 hours, 30 minutes, and 10 seconds. We would say, "Three thirty and ten seconds." Finally the third clock is 10 hours, 25 minutes, and 40 seconds. We would say, "Ten twenty-five and forty seconds."

Let's review what the race looks like when Ollie, Molly, and Sammy are all involved. They all three start on 12 noon (or 12 midday). Here's what happens:

- Ollie takes an hour to get from 12 to 1.
- Molly takes an hour to get from 12 clear around the clock to 12 again.
- Sammy rounds the clock every time Molly clicks off a minute. So in the time it takes Molly to get around from 12 to 12, Sammy has been around the clock 60 times! Wow!

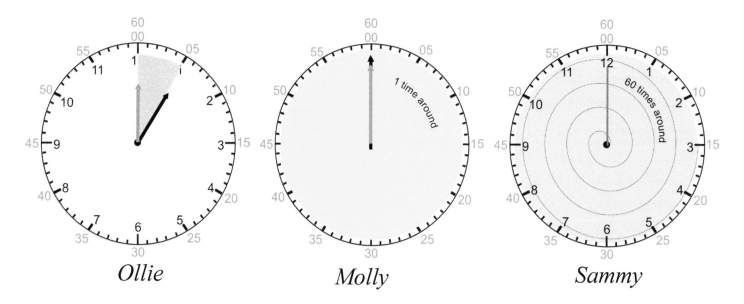

Ollie *Molly* *Sammy*

RULE: It takes 1 hour for Ollie to go from one number to the next. It takes 1 hour for Molly to go around the clock once. It takes 1 hour for Sammy to circle the clock 60 times.

Use resource 4.1 to practice writing in Molly's minutes.
Use resource 4.2 to have your child practice writing and reading the times shown.

Before moving on to the next chapter, please practice the arm motions and numbers that go with Molly's minutes. After all, analog clocks don't usually have minutes written out.

Minutes and Seconds

Just like Ollie sometimes is between numbers, so also are Molly and Sammy. Molly doesn't count minutes by fives all the time. Sometimes when you look at a clock, you will see Molly a bit past a number. Look at the examples below:

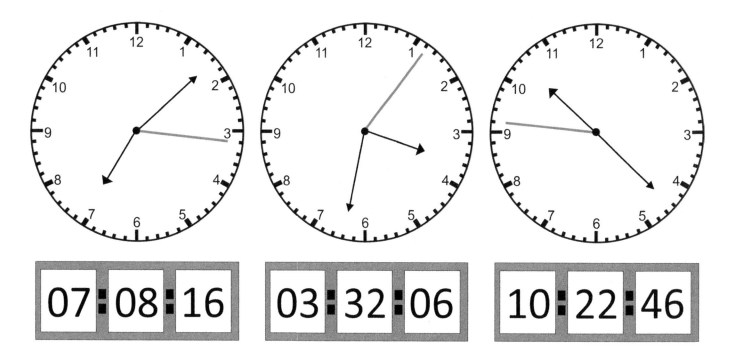

In the first clock, Molly passed 5 minute mark and ran past 3 more. So we can say, "5 - 6, 7, 8. It is 7:08. Sammy also blew past 15 seconds and is on the 16th second. So the time is "Seven oh eight and sixteen seconds."

On the second clock, we can see that Molly passed the 30 minute mark and is actually on 37. Sammy passed the 5 second mark and is now on 6. The time on that clock is "three thirty two and six seconds."

In the third clock, Molly passed the 20 minute mark and is now on 23. Sammy passed the 45 second mark and is now on 46. The time on this clock is "ten twenty-two and forty-six seconds."

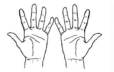 Please take the time to practice often with a toy clock until your child is comfortable naming the minutes between the numbers on the clock. One helpful exercise will be to ask your child to count on from any random number you name. Here's how to play:

Say, "5" and hold up two fingers. Your child will say, "5" and count on two more: "6, 7." The answer is 7 minutes.

Say, "30" and hold up 4 fingers. Your child will say, "30" and count on 4 more: "31, 32, 33, 34." Or hopefully he/she will just mentally add the 4 to the 30.

Say, "50" and hold up 1 finger. Your child will hopefully just say, "51." If not, he/she will say, "50, 51."

Say, "20" and hold up 3 fingers. Your child will say "20" and count on 3 more: "21, 22, 23." Or he/she may just say "23."

Fractions on the Clock

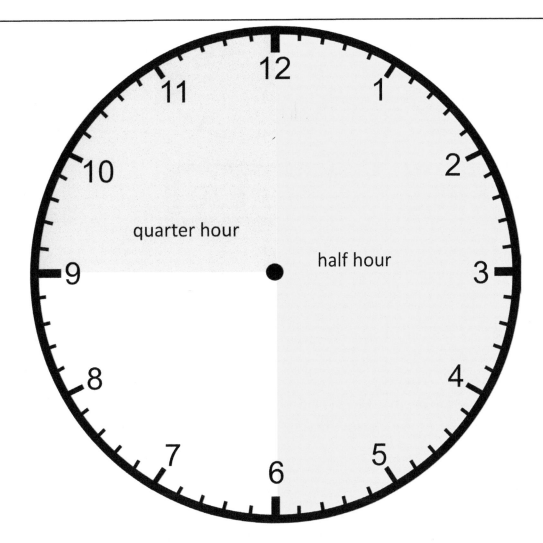

quarter hour

half hour

A. The Half Hour

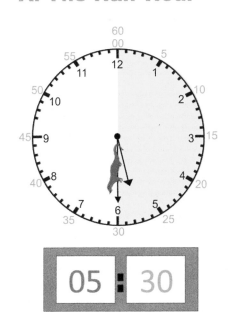

05 : 30

Half past the hour:

As Ollie waddles his way around the clock, whenever he is exactly halfway to the next hour, Molly will always, always be pointing to the 6. The 6 on the clock marks the halfway point, or the half of an hour. Ollie loves knowing exactly where Molly is at all times!

In the big clock above, the half hour is shown in yellow. When Ollie is halfway between 4 and 5, Molly will be on the 6. If he is halfway between 9 and 10, again, Molly will be pointing to the 6.

In the clock on the left, Ollie is between 5 and 6, and Molly is on 6. The time is 5:30. Another way to say it is, "Half past 5."

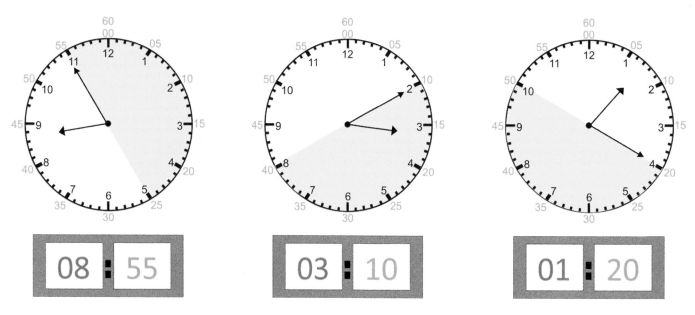

Above are three clocks showing three times. On each clock is also the yellow half hour graphic. This yellow graphic will show where Molly will be in another half an hour. For instance, in the first clock, the hands show 8:55. The yellow graphic shows that in another half hour, Molly will be pointing to the 5 and it will be 9:25.

The second clock says it is 3:10. In another half hour, Molly will be pointing to the 8 and the time will be 3:40. The third clock shows the time to be 1:20. In another half hour, Molly will be pointing to 10 and the time will be 1:50.

The interesting thing is each time you want to know what time it will be in half an hour, just know Molly will be pointing directly opposite where she is currently. Ollie might actually be at the next number, or past the next number, but it wouldn't be too hard to tell! If Molly passes the 12, Ollie will definitely be on the next hour! Otherwise, Ollie will be closer to the next hour, but not TO it yet.

RULE: When we speak of 30 minutes after the hour, we also say "Half past" the hour.

 Use R 6 to practice half hour increments.

B. The Quarter Hour

A quarter of something means a fourth of that thing. It means you start with a whole thing, cut it into four equal pieces, and then select one. There are 4 quarters in a dollar. There are four quarts in a gallon, interestingly enough. On a clock, there are four quarter hours in one hour. Each quarter hour is 15 minutes. The graphic on the big clock on the previous page shows the quarter hour in green.

Below are four clock faces. Each of them shows a quarter hour and Molly is racing ahead to mark the end of each quarter.

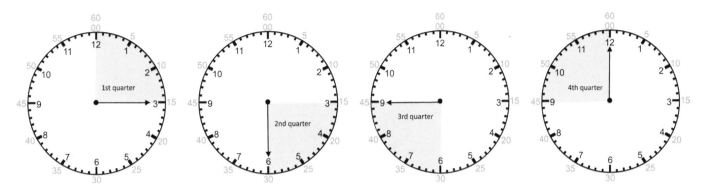

The first quarter of the hour ends when Molly reaches 3. See clock 1. The second quarter hour is on clock 2 and shows Molly reaching the 6. Hey! Isn't that where Molly points when she is marking the half hour? Yes it is! This means that two quarter hours is the same a one yellow half hour.

Clock 3 shows the third quarter hour with Molly pointing to 9. Finally, clock 4 shows the fourth quarter hour with Molly back at the starting gate: 12. The quarter hours are marked easily by drawing two lines to divide the clock face and also by skip counting by 3's: 3, 6, 9, and 12.

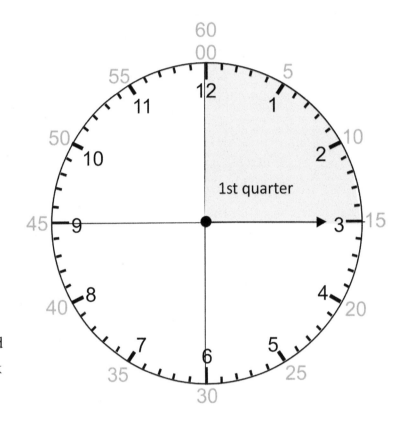

When Molly reaches the 3, we say it is quarter after whatever hour Ollie is on. When she reaches the 2nd quarter, Molly is pointing down and we say the hour and "thirty." When she is at the end of the third quarter, we say, [the hour] forty-five. At the end of the fourth quarter, we are back to hearing Molly say, "O'clock."

RULE: The four quarter hours end when Molly is at the 3, the 6, the 9, and the 12.

Use R 6 to practice quarter hour increments.

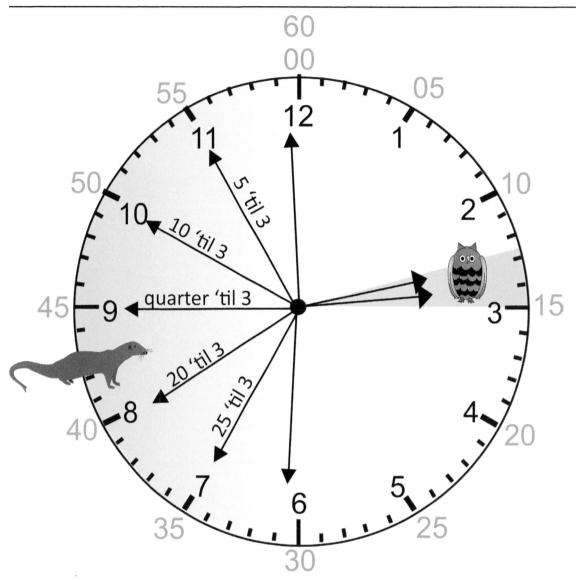

Minutes before the hour:

When we use digital clocks, telling time will always be Ollie's hour followed by Molly's minutes. Ollie's hour will always be the hour he just passed, while Molly's minutes will be the number of minutes she has passed on her way around the clock face. On an analog clock, talking about time can be more varied!

Sometimes people talk about time and like to mention how many minutes BEFORE Ollie's next hour we are. For instance, instead of saying, "It is 2:50," they might say, "It is 10 'til 3," (3 would be Ollie's next hour). What "It is 10 'til 3" really means is, "It is 10 minutes before Ollie reaches 3."

In the picture above, Ollie is sitting in an orange field that shows the time between 2:30 and 3:00. On the left, Molly is standing in another orange field that shows where she will be during that same period of time. Once Molly passes the 6, she is in the space where people might say how long until the next hour.

Notice the words on each of Molly's hands. There is everything from "25 'til 3" to "5 'til 3." But wait! Molly is not pointing to the orange 25 when we say, "It is 25 'til 3." She is pointing to the orange 35. Here is where it gets tricky.

Minute pairs:

In telling the time BEFORE the new hour, we have to use the orange numbers from the right side of the clock and pretend they are on the left also. Here is where being really sure of pairs of numbers on the clock comes in super handy! Here are the corresponding number pairs again:

55	05
50	10
45	15
40	20
35	25

The two columns of numbers are arranged just like they are on the clock. When you stretch your left arm up to point to the 55, your right arm, just opposite it, will be pointing to the 5 because 55 and 5 are a pair.

The next pair of numbers is 50 (left arm) and 10 (right arm). Continue on with the other pairs.

The clocks below are showing three different times. Under each clock, we describe the time both as minutes after the hour, and as minutes before the new hour.

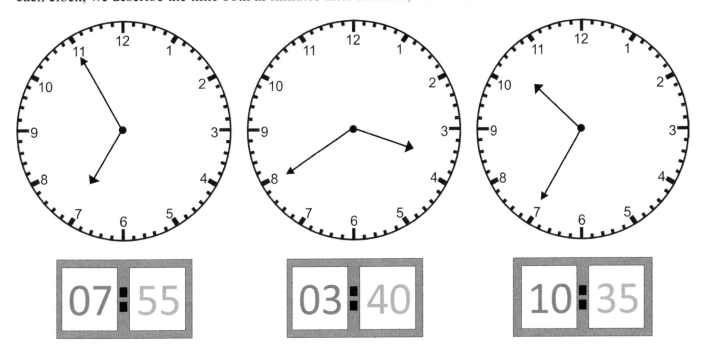

This clock says 7:55, which means 55 minutes AFTER 7. If we talk about minutes before the next hour, we would find 55's partner, the 5, and we'd say, "It is 5 'til 8."

This clock says 3:40, which means 40 minutes AFTER 3. If we talk about minutes before the next hour, we would find 40's partner, the 20, and we'd say, "It is 20 'til 4."

This clock says 10:35, which means 35 minutes AFTER 10. If we talk about minutes before the next hour, we would find 35's partner, the 25, and we'd say, "It is 25 'til 11."

Before putting pencil to paper, make sure you provide plenty of kinesthetic practice with identifying the orange partners on the clock.

Say, "Find 5." Your child will use his/her right arm to locate 5 on an "air clock."
Say, "Find 5's partner." Your child will locate 55 with left arm and will say, "55."

Say, "Find 15." Your child will use his/her right arm to locate 15 on an "air clock."
Say, "Find 15's partner." Your child will locate 45 with left arm and will say, "45."

Say, "Find 25." Your child will use his/her right arm to locate 25 on an "air clock."
Say, "Find 25's partner." Your child will locate 35 with left arm and will say, "35."

Say, "Find 10." Your child will use his/her right arm to locate 10 on an "air clock."
Say, "Find 10's partner." Your child will locate 50 with left arm and will say, "50."

Say, "Find 20." Your child will use his/her right arm to locate 20 on an "air clock."
Say, "Find 20's partner." Your child will locate 40 with left arm and will say, "40."

RULE: When we speak of time 'til, we rely on orange partners from the right side of the clock

 Use Resource 7 to practice time before the hour.

Future Time

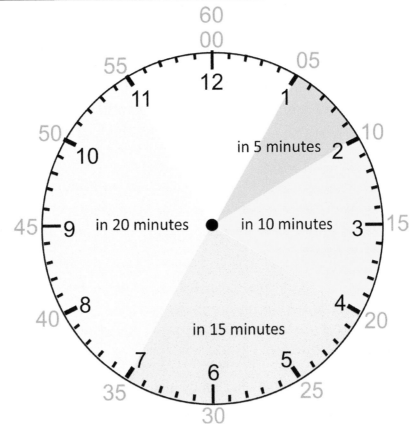

Now that we know how to tell time, let's move on to some interesting skills that will help as we talk about time in daily life. Say your family is planning to go to the park. Everyone is rushing around getting ready because Mom said, "We're leaving in 5 minutes!" You look at the clock and it looks like the clock below:

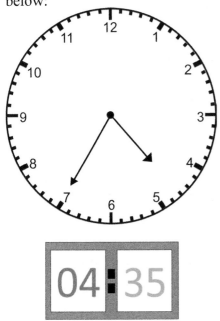

It is 4:35. If you are leaving in 5 minutes, you will need to jump ahead 5 minutes. Molly will be pointing to the 8 and the time will be 4:40. You can see this happening in the two clocks below:

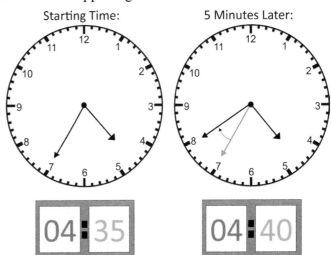

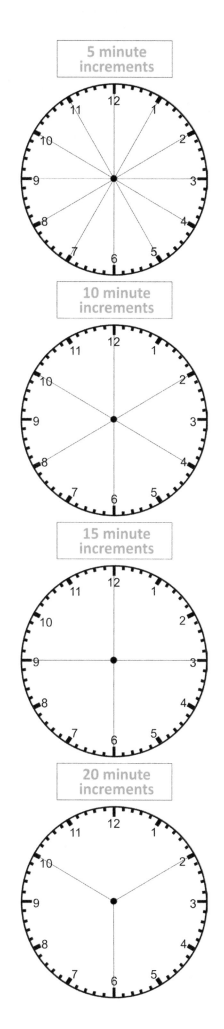

Spend time studying the clocks on the left. Each clock shows the shape of each of four increments of time: 5 minutes, 10 minutes, 15 minutes, and 20 minutes. Your child will already be familiar with the shape of 30 minutes and 15 minutes.

5 minute increments simply involve drawing lines from the center of the clock to each number. There are 12, 5-minute sections on a clock. When you want to know what time it will be in 5 minutes from now, just jump ahead to the next of Ollie's hours.

The second clock shows 10-minute increments. When you mark a clock for 10-minute increments, you draw lines to every other number. The numbers might be all of Ollie's hours that are even, OR it might be all of Ollie's hours that are odd, depending on where you start. In the clock on the left, we've drawn lines to all the numbers ending in zero: 10, 20, 30, 40, 50, and 60. There are six 10-minute slices in an hour.

If you want to know what time it will be in 10 minutes from now, just have Molly jump over one number and land on the one after it.

This clock shows quarter hours, or 15-minute increments of time. You can divide a clock face into quarters by first drawing a line from one number to its opposite (ex: 3, 9 or 4, 10, etc.) and then drawing another line exactly halfway between the numbers the first line connected. Or you can draw lines from the center, skipping over 2 numbers this time.

When you want to know what time it will be in 15 minutes, Molly will jump over two of Ollie's hours and land on the third one.

In this clock, we see 20-minute increments. You can mark 20's with your body by pretending to stand on the 6 and raising your arms to the 2 and the 10. When you want to know what time it will be in 20 minutes, Molly will take a giant leap over 3 of Ollie's hours!

Twenty minutes on the clock equal four 5-minutes or two 10-minute increments. There are three 20-minute slices in an hour.

Make it fun! Use toy clocks, one for each of you.

Set your clock to say 2:20. Have your child make his/her clock match yours.

Now say, "What time will it be in 5 minutes?" Your child will move Molly Minute to the right position and then will tell you the new time. "It will be 2:25." While your child is resetting his/her clock, move Molly on your clock to show the new time. You can compare your clocks.

Keep up this activity and keep it moving quickly so your child is not bored, but also not overly challenged. At first just ask about 5 minutes ahead, then move to asking the time 10 minutes in the future. Then move to 15 minutes, and finally 20 minutes.

When your child is comfortable with these games, begin to mix up the times. For example, start by asking for 5 minutes ahead, then ask the time 15 minutes ahead, then 30 minutes, then 10 minutes, etc.

Challenge Question:

Set your clock to a time of your choosing and ask, "What time will it be in 25 minutes?"

Of course we have not drawn a shape for 25-minute increments! See what your child comes up with. One option is to jump ahead 20 minutes and then add another 5 minutes ahead. Another option is to jump ahead 30 minutes and then reverse back 5 minutes to the correct time.

Rather than just telling your child the answer, discuss it, ask him/her questions, and hopefully your child will solve the riddle on his/her own!

> RULE: We can tell future time by having Molly skip ahead the right number of minutes.

Use Resource 8 to practice future times.

Elapsed Time

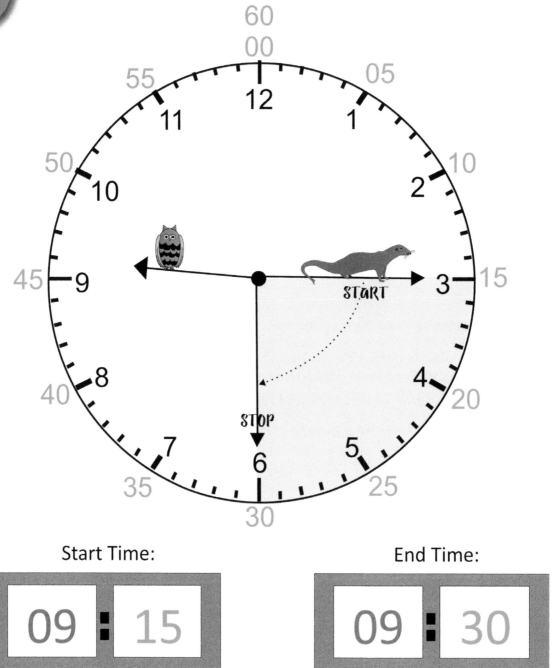

Start Time:

09 : 15

End Time:

09 : 30

Sometimes when we are making plans with a friend, we speak of a time we will start an activity and a time we will finish. For example, your friend might say, "Let's go run around the track. We can start at 9:15 and we'll be done at 9:30 in plenty of time to go to the park."

When we speak of a start and finish time, it is helpful to understand how much time the activity will take. Look at the clock above. The kids started running at 9:15 and finished at 9:30. How much time did they spend running? They ran for a quarter hour - or for 15 minutes. The time that elapsed was 15 minutes.

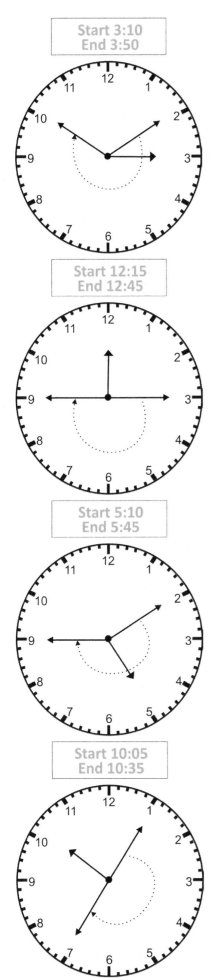

Start 3:10
End 3:50

Start 12:15
End 12:45

Start 5:10
End 5:45

Start 10:05
End 10:35

A. Less than an hour

When we are figuring elapsed time and it is less than an hour, our shapes will come in handy! Skip counting by 5's or 10's will also come in handy.

Let's look at some clocks. In the first clock, the start time was 3:10 and the end time was 3:50. There are a couple of ways to figure out how much time passed. One way is to see the shape of Molly's arms. From the 2 around to the 10 we can see two 20-minute shapes. The first one goes from the 2 to the 6 and the second one from the 6 to the 10. 20 and 20 make 40 elapsed minutes.

Or you might want to count by 5's or 10's. Starting on the 2, count each of Ollie's hours by 5's: 5, 10, 15, 20, 25, 30, 35, 40. Or you can take the ending minutes and subtract the starting minutes from it. Each of these ways will result in 40 minutes elapsed.

In the second clock, the starting time is 12:15 and the ending time is 12:45. If you picture where those minutes are on the clock, it might remind you of holding your arms out straight from your body. Those arms are marking a 30 minute shape, aren't they? You can skip count, you can just look at the shape of 30 minutes, or you can subtract the start minutes from the ending minutes. All will result in 30 minutes elapsed time.

In the third clock, we are starting at 5:10 and ending at 5:45. I can see a 20-minute shape followed by a 15-minute shape. Your child might want to add two 20-minute shapes and subtract out the missing 5 minutes; he/she might start with a 30-minute shape and add the extra 5 minutes; he/she might want to skip count, or subtract the starting minutes from the ending minutes. All these options will result in 35 minutes of elapsed time.

In the last clock, see if your child notices right away the shape the two minute hands make. This time have your child walk you through the various ways to figure out elapsed time.

B. More than an hour

Sometimes elapsed time is for more than an hour. When we figure out how much time elapsed in those situations, first we figure how many numbers Ollie passed, then we figure out how many more minutes Molly passed.

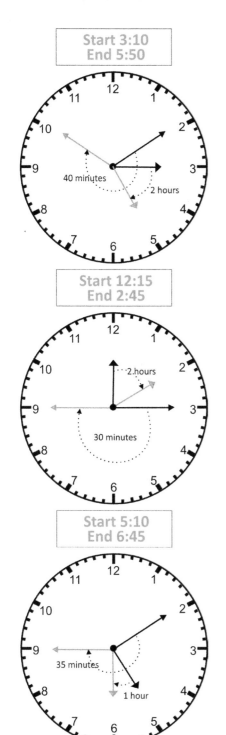

40 minutes

2 hours

2 hours

30 minutes

35 minutes

1 hour

In these clocks, the time each activity took more than an hour. Let's look at each one and figure out how much time elapsed. In each picture, the black hands show start time, while the gray hands show the end times.

In clock one, we start at 3:10 and end at 5:50. You will move the Ollie two places, or two hours. You will move Molly 40 minutes. Time elapsed is 2 hours and 40 minutes. You can solve for elapsed time in several ways like before. You can move the hands on the clock while you count, you can look at the shapes made by the start and stop locations, or you can subtract the start time from the end time.

In the second clock, we start at 12:15 and end at 2:45. Ask your child what his/her preferred way is for solving the elapsed time question. You can move Ollie on a toy clock, noting that he moves two hours. Then you can move Molly from the 3 to the 9. Arms straight out to the sides means that you are showing a 30 minute spread. However you decide it makes most sense to solve the problem, the answer is that 2 hours and 30 minutes elapsed.

In clock 3, you can see that Ollie only moved forward one hour. Molly, on the other hand, moved a half hour and five more minutes - or 35 minutes. Elapsed time is a total of 1 hour and 35 minutes.

To give your child extra practice, and as long as his/her attention is engaged, make up pretend events, naming start and end times and have your child use a toy clock to figure out elapsed time.

RULE: There are different ways to figure elapsed time. Use what makes the most sense to you.

Use Resource 9 to practice elapsed times.

End Times

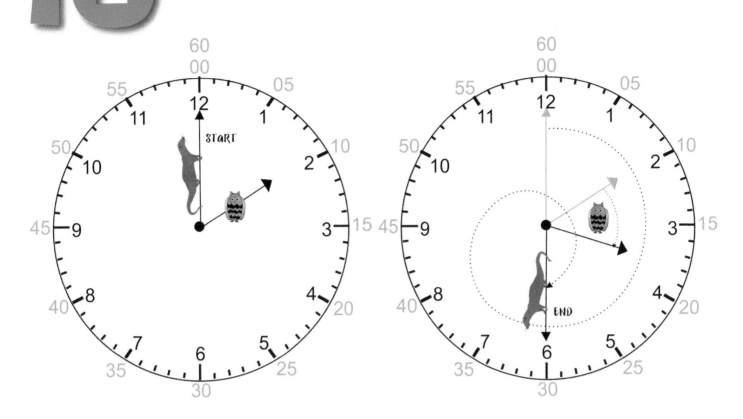

It will come in handy to know how to calculate end times. Say, for example, your dad asks you when you will be home from practice. You know practice starts at 2:00 and lasts for an hour and a half. You can picture a clock in your mind for this. Ollie will start on the 2:00 and will travel to the 3 and half way to the 4. Molly, on the other hand, will go around the clock face from 12:00 to 12:00 and then will go another half hour and end up pointing to the 6.

Look at the clocks above. The first clock shows the time practice starts. The second clock shows the same start time with the hands in gray. It also shows that Ollie and Molly each traveled an hour and a half - the length of practice. The black hands on the clock show the time practice ends: 3:30.

You can solve for end times by simply adding hours together and adding minutes together. Usually this will work. In this case, practice starts at 2. You would add the one hour to the 2 to get 3. You would then add the 30 minutes to the 00 to arrive at 3:30.

It isn't that simple when your start time is close to the end of the hour, however. For example, say that on Saturday, your start time for practice is 10:45. Practice still lasts an hour and a half. You can add one hour to the 10, but in order to add Molly's minutes, you will pass the 12, pushing Ollie to the next hour! Let's look at this on the clocks.

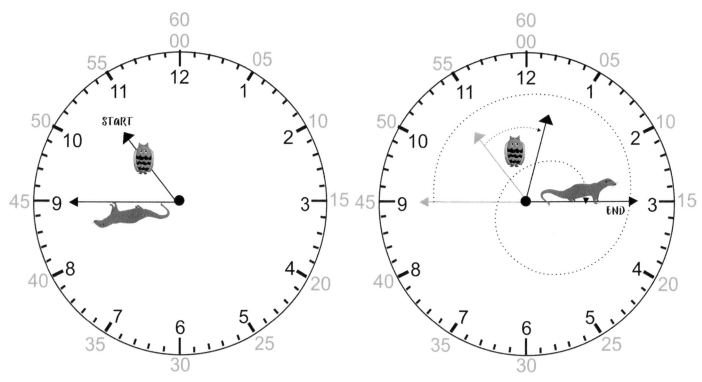

Again, the first clock shows the starting time. Notice that Ollie is close to the 11. This is because it is already 45 minutes after 10:00. The second clock shows the starting time in gray and again shows the one and a half hour practice. Ollie moves an hour, which brings him almost to the 12. Then he continues for another half hour, which brings him past the 12. Molly simply circles the clock one and a half times. The time practice ends is 12:15.

Using toy clocks, practice these scenarios:

1. The movie starts at 3:30 and lasts for 2 hours. What time will the movie end? [5:30]

2. We started lunch at 12:10 and it lasted for 45 minutes. What time did we finish? [12:55]

3. The basketball game started at 7:15 and lasted an hour and 40 minutes. What time was it over? [8:55]

4. We started making cookies at 10:00. We baked four batches that each took 10 minutes. What time were we finished with all the cookies? [add 40 minutes to 10:00 to get 10:40]

5. I started doing my homework at 4:15 and it took 35 minutes. What time was I finished? [4:50]

A good rule of thumb is to look at the minutes for both the start time and the length of the activity. If they will equal 60 or more minutes, you will add another hour to Ollie's hours.

RULE: When calculating end time, add the minutes. If they total 60 or more, add another hour to the end time.

Use Resource 10 to practice calculating end times.

Estimating Time

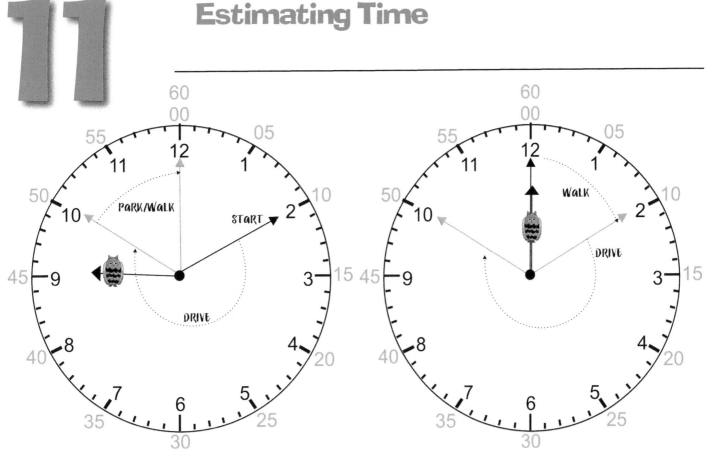

A wonderful skill to learn is how to estimate time. Sounds super boring, but it will help make life smoother for you! Here is an example of what it means to estimate time. A flea market your family wants to go to is open from 10-12 in the morning. The market is 40 minutes away. If you want to have both hours for browsing, it is wise to make a plan in which you estimate the time it will take to drive, park, and walk into the market. Here is a sample plan:

1. Drive to market	40 minutes
2. Park and walk	10 minutes
3. Shop	2 hours
4. Walk to car	10 minutes
5. Drive home	40 minutes

In this case, start with the 2 hours the market will take. Now add 40 + 10 to calculate the time you need *before* 10:00. If you leave home at 9:10, you will have 40 minutes to drive, and 10 minutes to park and walk before the market opens. If you leave the market at 12 noon, you will take 10 + 40 minutes (50 minutes) to get home. You will reach home at 12:50.

Look at the two clocks above. The first clock shows the time it will take you to drive, park, and walk. The second clock shows the time you need to get home after the market is over. That clock starts at noon when the market closes, and takes you the 50 minutes you will need to get back to the car and drive home.

1. We get out of school at 3:00 and have dinner at 5:30. Sometime after school and before dinner, I need to do my chores and homework. My homework usually takes 40 minutes and my chores take 25. I also want to have a little snack after school before I start working. I estimate snack time taking 15 minutes. I also want to have free time before dinner. When should I start snack in order to finish it, my homework, and my chores before dinner?

Use a toy clock if desired. Preferably, ask your child what he/she thinks is the easiest way to make this plan and go with that.

[Add the times the three activities will take to complete. 15+40+25 = 80 minutes. There are 60 minutes in an hour. 80 - 60 leaves 20 minutes. I will need 1 hour and 20 minutes to complete all three activities. Move the hands on the clock back an hour, then move them back 20 more minutes. If I start at 4:10, I can be finished by 5:30. If I want free time before dinner, I will need to begin my activities earlier. For example, if I want an hour of free time, I would need to begin at 3:10.]

2. Our school play starts at 6:00 tonight. We need to figure out what time we should leave in order to drive there, park, walk into the auditorium, find our seats, and get settled without being rushed or late. What is the best way to make a plan?

Questions to answer:
How long will it take to drive there?
How long should we allow to find a parking place?
How long should we allow to walk to the auditorium, get tickets, and find our seats?

[This time you will start at 6:00 and go backwards the number of minutes each activity takes.]

RULE: When estimating times, take into account all the activities involved and how long they will take.

Use Resource 11 to practice estimating times.

Part I - Time Resources

In the pages following are resources for you to use with your child to practice telling time. One sheet may or may not be enough practice. If you feel your child needs more practice, simply provide more practice using a toy clock, or a real clock. Consider a watch your child can wear and refer as you go about your daily routine.

Following this page are two pages of blank clock faces you can print and use to create additional practice as needed.

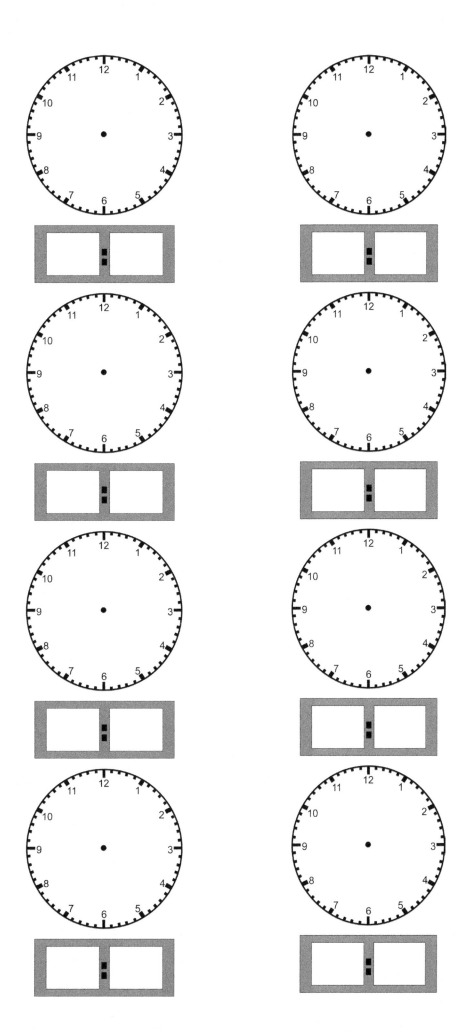

R-1 - Writing Times on Analog and Digital Clocks

There are pairs of clocks below. One clock will show a time. Make the other clock say the same time.

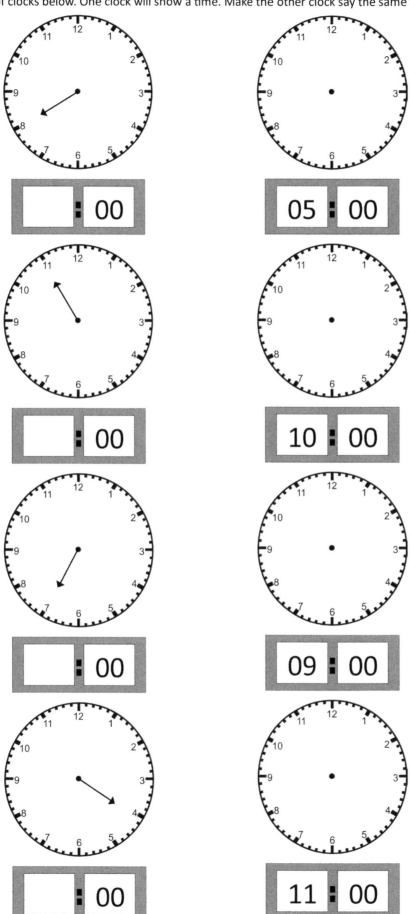

Right-Brained Time, Money, & Measurement © 2017 Sarah Major, Child1st Publications, www.child1st.com.

R-1.2 - Practice with A.M. and P.M.

For each activity, give a time and use a.m. or p.m.

1. I get up on a school day. _____

2. I have lunch. _____

3. I do homework. _____

4. We have recess. _____

5. We have dinner. _____

6. I eat breakfast. _____

7. We get out of school. _____

8. I leave for school. _____

9. I go to bed. _____

10. I do my chores. _____

R-2 - Practice Writing Hours and Minutes

Draw hands on each analog clock to show the same time as the digital clock.

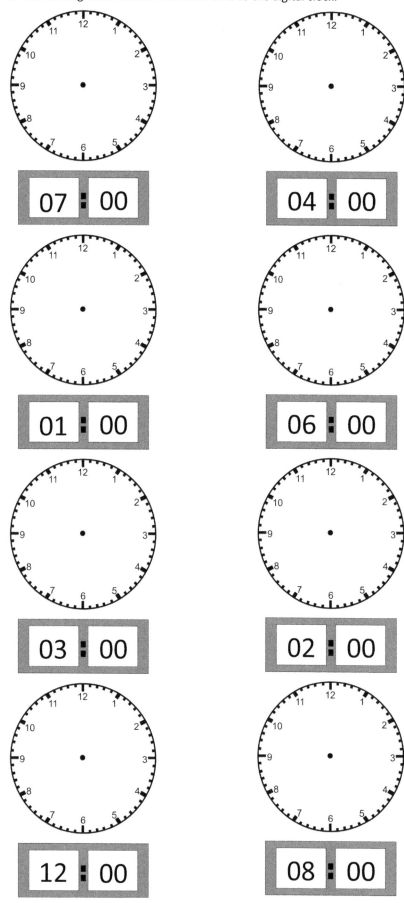

Right-Brained Time, Money, & Measurement © 2017 Sarah Major, Child1st Publications, www.child1st.com.

R-4.1 - Practice Writing Molly's Minutes

There are pairs of clocks below. One clock will show a time. Make the other clock say the same minutes.

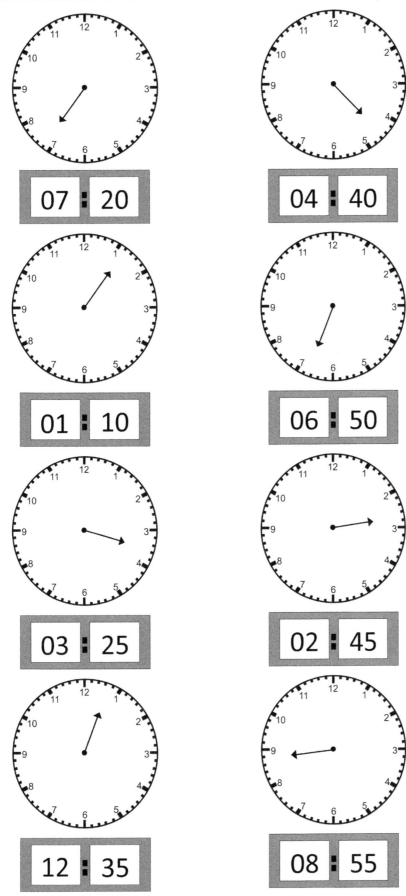

R-4.2 - Practice Writing Hours, Minutes, and Seconds

There are pairs of clocks below. One clock will show a time. Make the other clock say the same time.

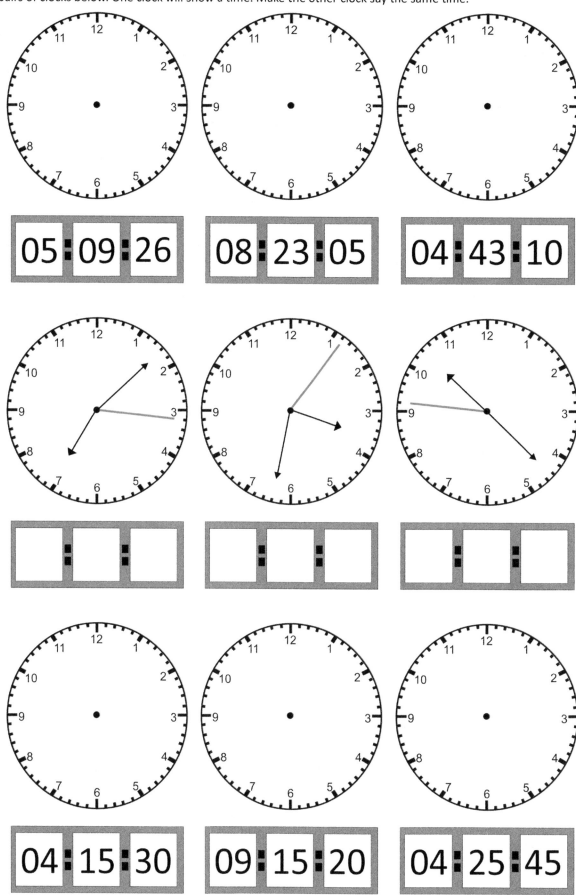

Right-Brained Time, Money, & Measurement © 2017 Sarah Major, Child1st Publications, www.child1st.com.

R-6.1 - Practice Writing a Half Hour Later

There are pairs of clocks below. On the analog clocks, draw a Molly Minute hand showing one half hour later than the clocks show right now. Write the new minutes in the digital clock below each analog clock.

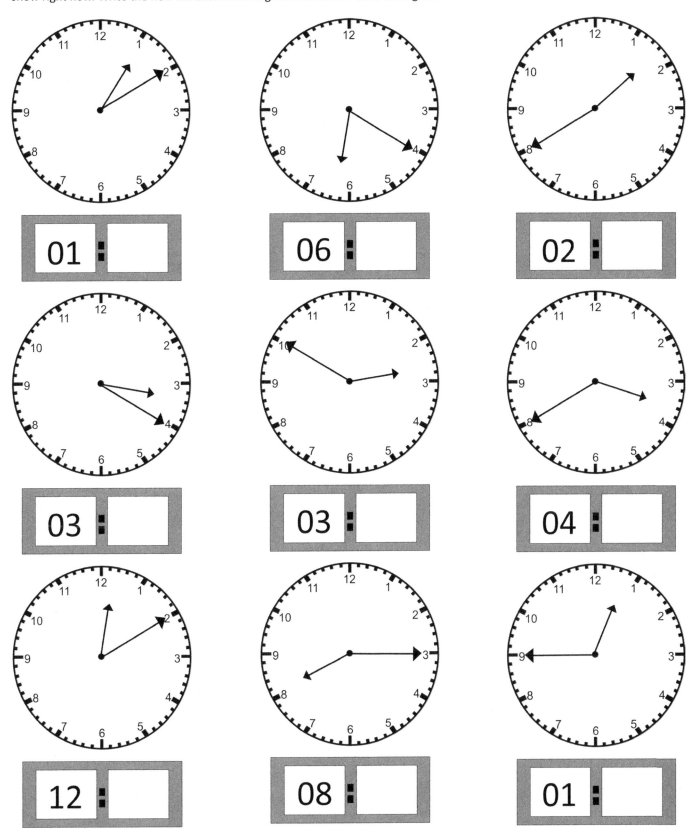

R-6.2 - Practice Writing a Quarter Hour Later

There are pairs of clocks below. On the analog clocks, draw a Molly Minute hand showing one quarter hour later than the clocks show right now. Write the new minutes in the digital clock below each analog clock.

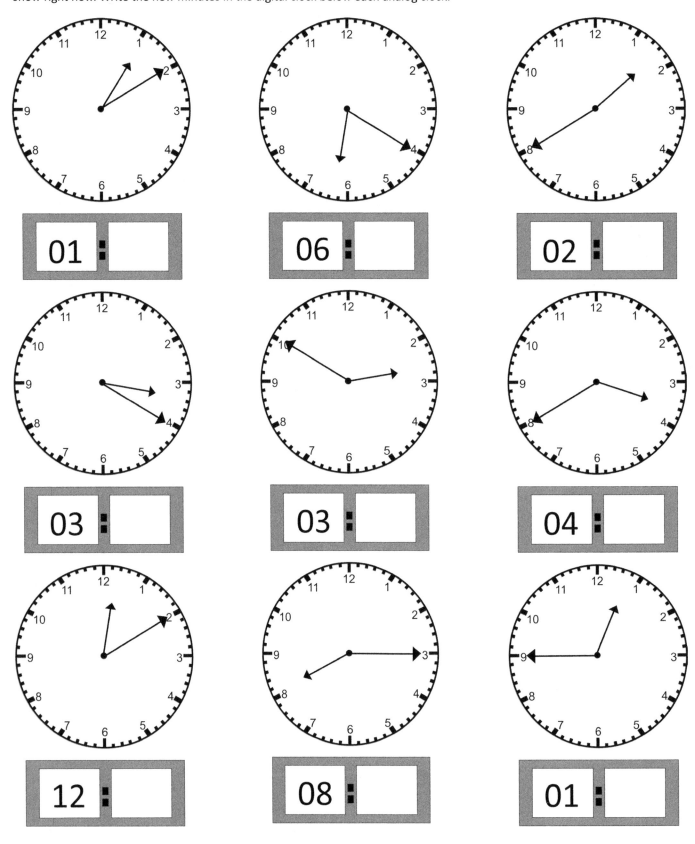

Right-Brained Time, Money, & Measurement © 2017 Sarah Major, Child1st Publications, www.child1st.com.

R-7 - Practice Time 'Til

Each clock below is missing Molly Minute. Read the time 'til above each clock and draw Molly for each clock.

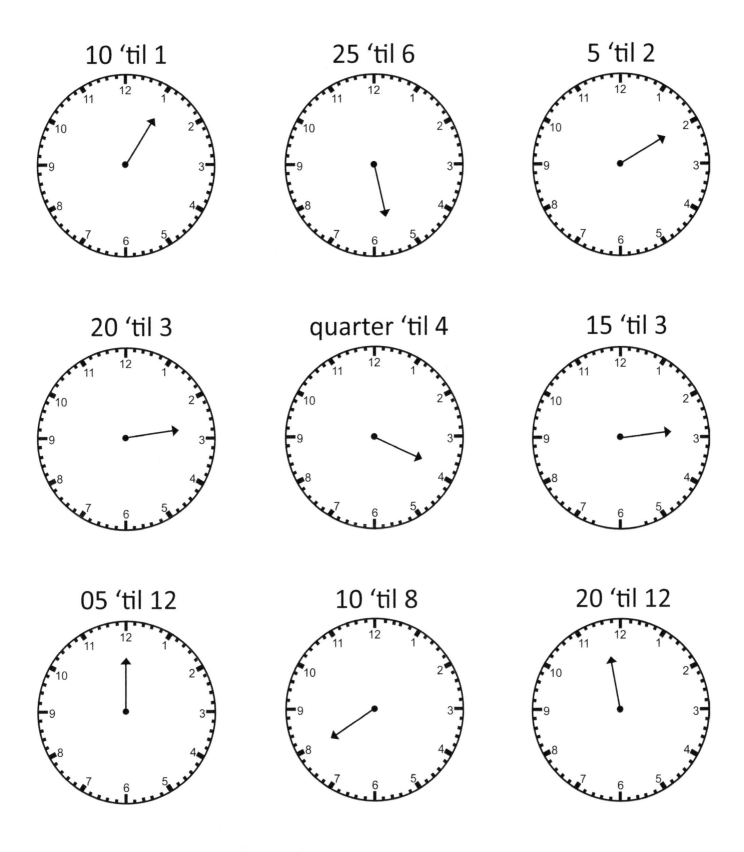

10 'til 1   25 'til 6   5 'til 2

20 'til 3   quarter 'til 4   15 'til 3

05 'til 12   10 'til 8   20 'til 12

R-8 - Practice Future Time

Each clock shows a time and also say future minutes. Draw a Molly hand on each clock showing where she will be in the future minutes.

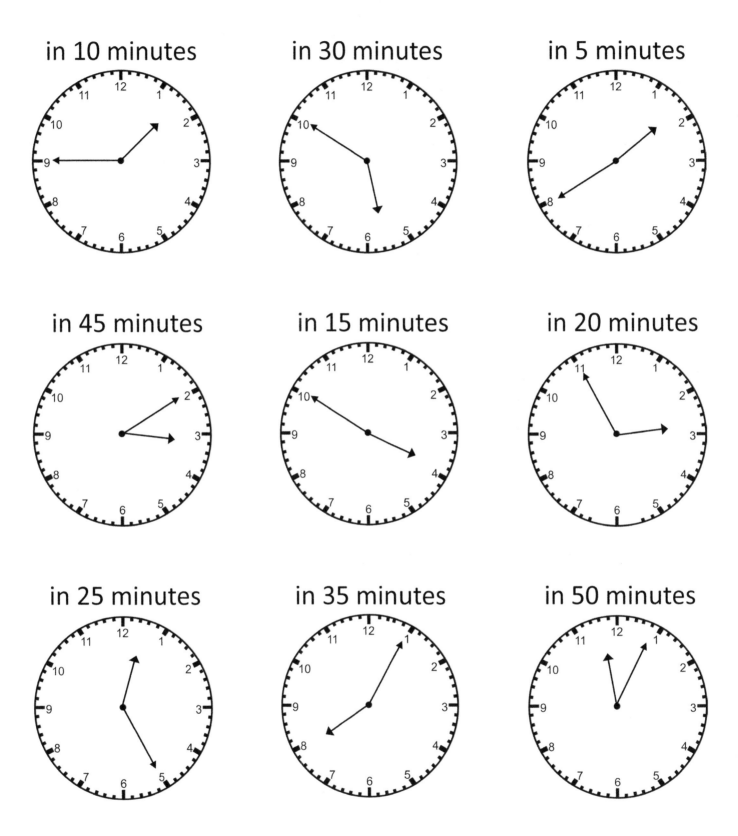

in 10 minutes   in 30 minutes   in 5 minutes

in 45 minutes   in 15 minutes   in 20 minutes

in 25 minutes   in 35 minutes   in 50 minutes

 Right-Brained Time, Money, & Measurement © 2017 Sarah Major, Child1st Publications, www.child1st.com.

R-9.1 - Practice Elapsed Time - Under an Hour

Each clock shows a time and also say future minutes. Draw a Molly hand on each clock showing where she will be in the future minutes. Also draw a new Ollie (hour) hand to show that he has moved as well. Write the future times in the digital clocks.

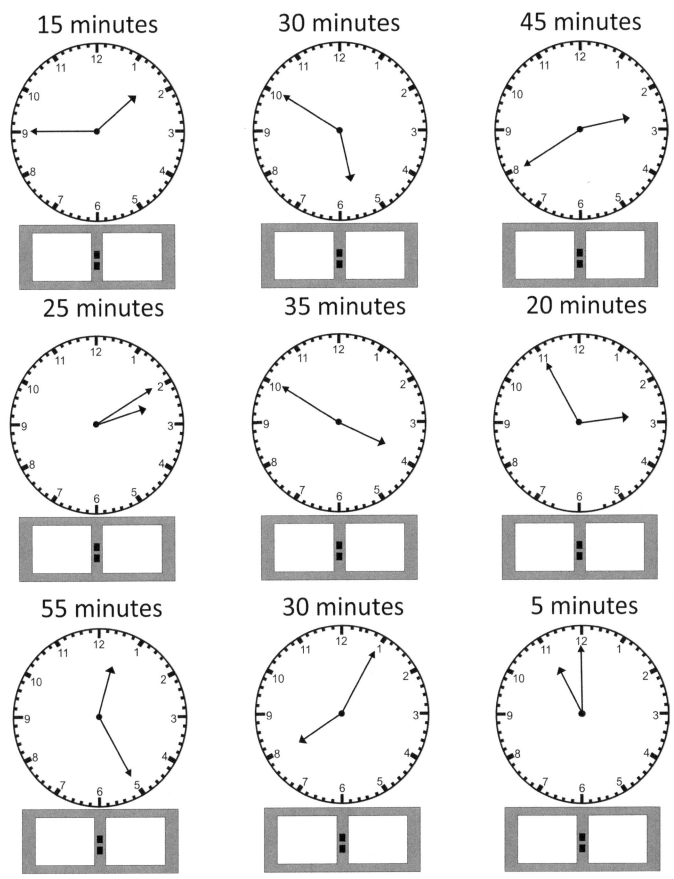

15 minutes   30 minutes   45 minutes

25 minutes   35 minutes   20 minutes

55 minutes   30 minutes   5 minutes

R-9.2 - Practice Elapsed Time - Over an Hour

Each clock shows a time and also give future minutes. Draw a Molly hand on each clock showing where she will be at the future time. Also draw a new Ollie (hour) hand to show that he has moved as well.

1 hour & 15 minutes
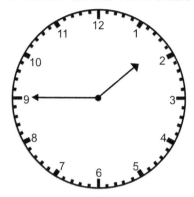

1 hour & 30 minutes
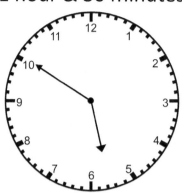

1 hour & 45 minutes
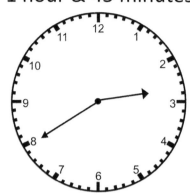

1 hour & 25 minutes

1 hour & 35 minutes

1 hour & 20 minutes

1 hour & 55 minutes
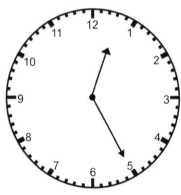

1 hour & 30 minutes

1 hour & 5 minutes

R-10 - Practice End Times

Each clock shows a starting time. There are events that take time. First add the minutes used and calculate the ending time. Draw hands on each clock in a contrasting color to show the ending times.

At 6:00 we left for the football game. It took 5 minutes to get ready and get in the car, 20 minutes to drive, 10 minutes to park and walk to the stadium. What time is it now?

At quarter to 1:00, I started taking care of our dogs. It took 10 minutes to feed them, 20 minutes to walk them, and then 30 minutes to brush them down. What time was it when I finished all this?

At 2:30, Tom and I started yard work. It took 40 minutes to mow, and 30 minutes to weed the flower beds. What time is it now?

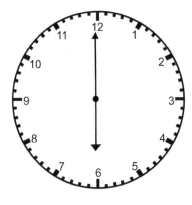
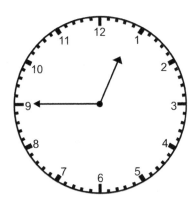
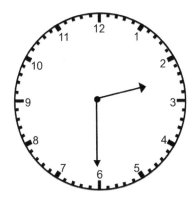

At 4:30, Sue and Jeff began to cook. It took 20 minutes to grill hamburgers, 15 minutes to make a salad, and 10 minutes to set the table. What time was it when dinner was ready?

At 1:00 we drove to the store. We spent 10 minutes in produce, 5 minutes in meats, 15 minutes in line to pay. What time did we finish at the store?

At 7:30 I started getting ready for school. I spent 5 minutes brushing my teeth, 10 minutes getting dressed, 10 minutes eating breakfast. What time was it when I was ready for school?

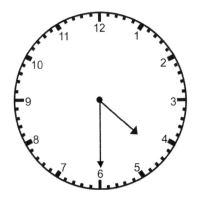

R-11 - Practice Estimating Time

For each story, first estimate the time each task will take. Next, add the times. The first clock will show the starting time. Once you have figured out how much time all the tasks will take, write the times in the spaces provided, then draw hands on the second clock showing ending times.

You have homework in three subjects, reading, math, and science. Estimate how much time you need for each subject. You start at 4:00. What time will you be finished?
The first clock shows the start time. Draw hands to show the end time on the second clock.

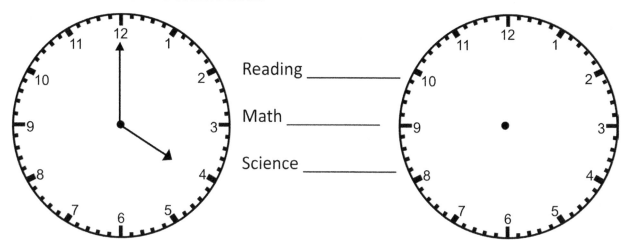

Reading _____

Math _____

Science _____

You are helping clean house on Saturday. Your jobs are going to dust, empty the trashcans, and empty the dishwasher. Estimate how much time you need for each task. What time will you be finished? Draw the hands on the second clock to show when you will be finished.

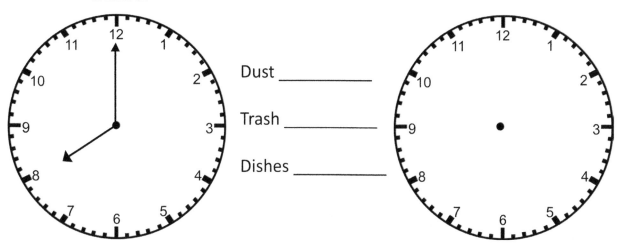

Dust _____

Trash _____

Dishes _____

Part II - Money

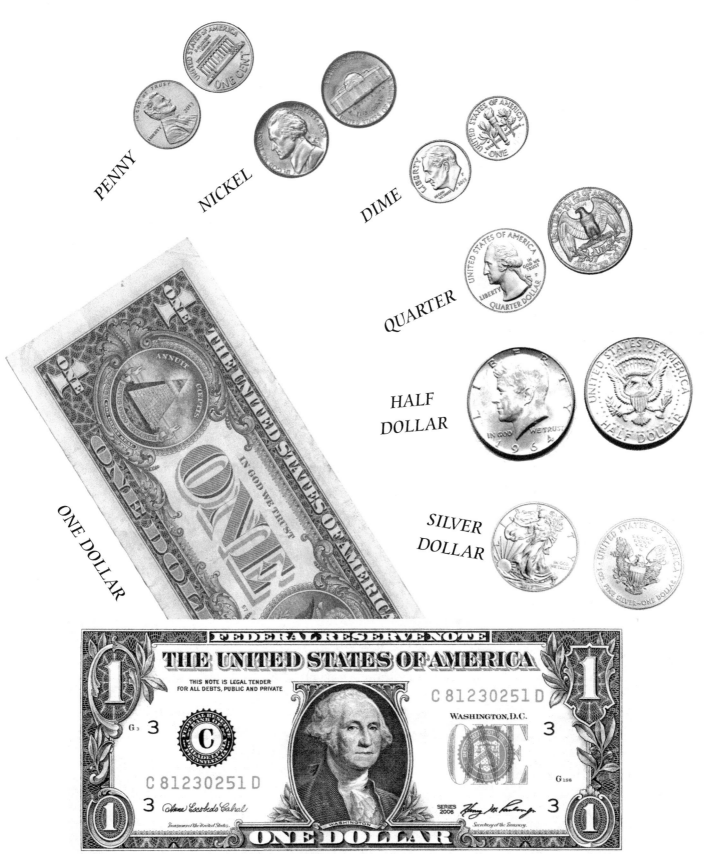

PENNY

NICKEL

DIME

QUARTER

HALF
DOLLAR

SILVER
DOLLAR

ONE DOLLAR

The Penny

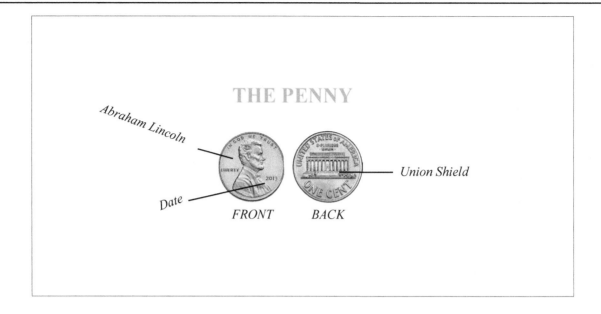

THE PENNY

Abraham Lincoln

Date

Union Shield

FRONT   BACK

About the Penny

History

The penny was the first currency of any kind authorized by the United States over 200 years ago. The first penny was struck at a private mint in 1787 and was much larger than our penny today. There have been 11 different designs over the years. President Abraham Lincoln was put on the penny for his 100th birthday in 1909!

The penny has always symbolized freedom and the spirit of our country. Lincoln fought to preserve a united country and so in 2010, the back of the penny was changed from the Lincoln Memorial to the design showing "the preservation of the union." This design shows a union shield that has 13 stripes representing the first 13 colonies. "E Pluribus Unum" is written at the top of the shield and means, "Out of many, One." In Latin, E means "from" or "out of," Pluribus means "more" and Unum means "one." E Pluribus Unum refers to 13 colonies coming together to form one nation, and it also speaks to America being the melting pot of people from many nations. Together we are the people of the United States of America.

What it buys

100 years ago, you could buy a candy stick for a penny, but today you would need about 19¢ to buy a similar candy stick! Count out 19 pennies so you can see how much money you would need to pay for a stick of candy.

On the right are some Skittles packs. Each of those packs costs 61¢. Can you count out enough pennies to buy one pack?

Shopping with the Penny

Practice paying for the following items by counting out pennies to match the price of each item. Notice that the sign ¢ means "cent" or penny.

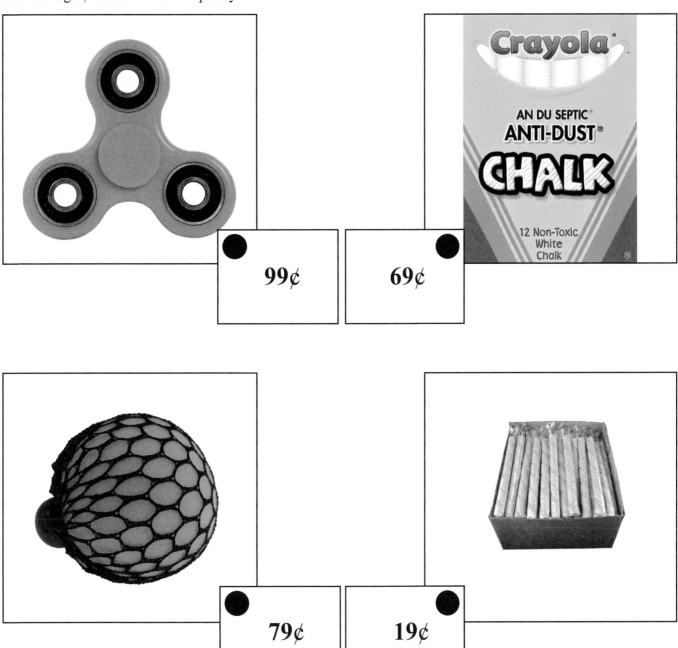

What do you think about shopping with pennies? Do you think you would like to carry hundreds of pennies around with you when you go shopping? No? You wouldn't? Well, have I got great news for you! After you do the penny activity, move on to our next chapter - Nickels. You're going to love nickels!

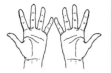 Use Resource 1 to practice shopping with pennies.

The Nickel

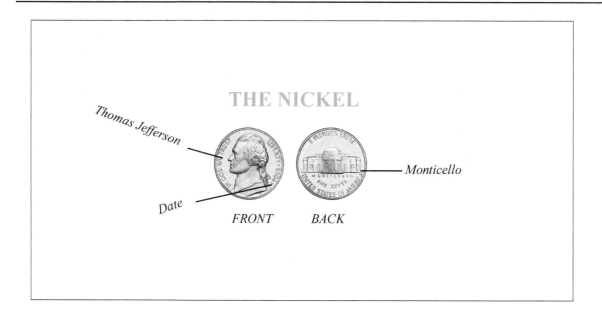

THE NICKEL

Thomas Jefferson

Date

FRONT

BACK

Monticello

About the Nickel

History

The history of the nickel is very interesting. The first nickel was printed right after the Civil War when there was a shortage of gold and silver and the demand for a 5 cent coin was in great demand. The first nickel was minted in 1866. The name "nickel" comes from the type of metal that is used. Actually a nickel is 75% copper and only 25% nickel, but the name stuck. There have been several nickel designs over the years: the shield nickel, the liberty head nickel, the buffalo nickel, and two versions of the Jefferson nickel.

Even after dimes and quarters became popular, nickels continued to be the most popular coin because of how useful it was. Beginning in 1886, and for 76 years, a bottle of Coke cost a nickel, and many coin-operated machines took nickels, too. Vending machines, jukeboxes, slot machines, and nickel theatres, called Nickelodeons, all were a nickel.

What it buys

When you were practicing shopping using pennies, it would have been really helpful to have nickels to use, too! Why? Because you can use 1 nickel instead of 5 pennies! Instead of carrying around 5 pennies, you can carry one nickel!

If something costs 10 cents, you could either count out 10 pennies, or you could use 2 nickels! Two coins instead of 10!

Now, let's get some practice changing pennies for nickels. For this activity, you will need a large pile of pennies and a smaller pile of nickels. Make stacks of 5 pennies in each stack. When you have finished all the pennies, put 1 nickel by each stack of 5 pennies.

Point to each nickel in turn and count by fives as you do. Write down the number you end on. For example, if you have 15 nickels, you would count by 5's like this: 5, 10, 15, 20, 25, 30, 35, 40, 45, 50, 55, 60, 65, 70, 75. Your 15 nickels are worth 75 pennies. Without having to count your stacks of pennies, you know you also have 75¢ worth of pennies. Wow!

Shopping with pennies and nickels

Now the fun begins! Let's use the same toys we were working with last time, but this time, let's use mostly nickels and just fill in with pennies when we have to. The first toy costs 99¢. Let's start counting out nickels until we are very close to the 99¢, but without going over. Put one nickel down each time you say a number: "5, 10, 15, 20, 25, 30, 35, 40, 45, 50, 55, 60, 65, 70, 75, 80, 85, 90, 95." We'd better stop! Now let's add pennies

until we reach exactly 99¢. "96, 97, 98, 99." How many nickels and pennies equal 99¢. We used 19 nickels and 4 pennies instead of using 99 pennies like last time!

The chalk box costs 79¢. Start counting by 5's, laying a nickel down each time you say a number. "5, 10, 15, 20, 25, 30, 35, 40, 45, 50, 55, 60, 65, 70, 75." Now add pennies as you continue to count: "76, 77, 78, 79." Count how many nickels you used, and then how many pennies you used. 15 nickels and 4 pennies is the same as 79 pennies! To buy the chalk, you would only have to carry 19 coins - instead of 79 coins!

The squishy ball costs 69¢. Let's count by 5's and place a nickel on the table each time we say a number. Just remember to stop before reaching 69. "5, 10, 15, 20, 25, 30, 35, 40, 45, 50, 55, 60, 65." Now count on, laying down pennies until you reach 69: "66, 67, 68, 69." How many nickels and pennies did you use? 13 nickels and 4 pennies instead of 69 pennies!

Finally, one stick candy costs 19¢. Count out nickels: "5, 10, 15." Now count on with pennies: "16, 17, 18, 19." How many coins? Only 7! Did you notice that in each case you only used 4 pennies? Why is this? (Each price ends in a 9, which is 4 more than the last number that ends in 5 in the price.)

Now that you have shopped with pennies by themselves, and also with pennies and nickels, tell us which you liked better? Why? Which was easier?

A quick tip for remembering the name "nickel" and how many pennies it is worth - hold up one hand with your fingers spread out. Now, make a fist with your hand and say (with a smile) "I'm going to give you a nickel sandwich!"

If you said you liked using nickels and pennies together, just wait until next time! You will adore dimes!

RULE: One nickel is worth as much as five pennies.

Use Resource 2 to practice shopping with pennies and nickels.

The Dime

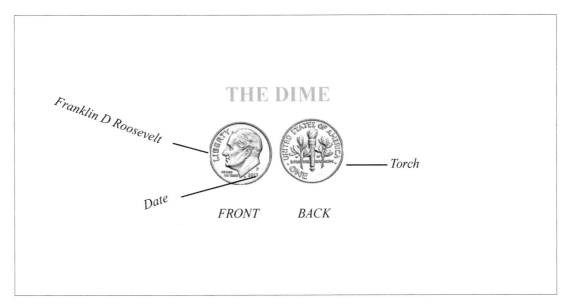

THE DIME

Franklin D Roosevelt

Date

FRONT

Torch

BACK

About the Dime

History

The first dime was minted in 1796, but interestingly enough, the United States had to borrow a coin machine for the four years until they could build a mint. The dime was intended to be worth exactly 1/10 of the value of the silver coin valued at a dollar. The name "dime" comes from the old French "disme," which means a tenth.

The first five designs of the coin have carried the message of freedom and included figures that represented liberty. The current dime showing President Franklin D Roosevelt was designed in 1946. President Roosevelt was honored because he led our country through the great depression and World War II, both events which brought much suffering to the nation. The back of the dime shows a torch in the middle that represents liberty, an olive branch on the left representing peace, and an oak branch on the right representing strength. The symbols on this coin honor the victorious end of World War II.

President Roosevelt was also honored because of the work he did to raise money and support for those suffering with polio. President Roosevelt was struck with this crippling disease at age 39 and spent the rest of his life in a wheelchair, paralyzed from his waist down. He founded The March of Dimes to raise money to help polio victims, and to research and develop a vaccine that would prevent polio outbreaks. The organization was called the march of dimes because Roosevelt thought it was better to ask millions of people for a dime than to ask a few rich people to contribute money.

RULE: One dime is worth the same as two nickels or ten pennies.

Look at the money picture below. At the very top is the dime. It is worth 10¢. Two nickels are also worth 10¢, and so are 10 pennies. When you look at the 10 pennies, does it remind you of the 10 fingers on your hands? You can pretend that the two nickels represent your two hands, and the pennies represent your 10 fingers, and the dime is your two hands clasped together. It is pretty easy to remember a dime when you. say, "It's time for a dime!" as you clasp your hands together.

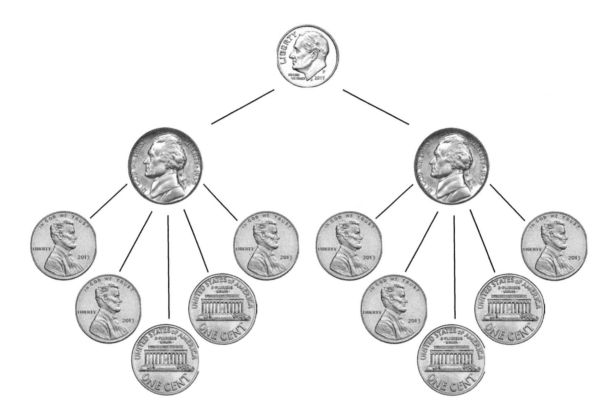

When you were practicing shopping using pennies and nickels, it would have been really helpful to have dimes! Remember that at first you counted out all pennies? Boy, that took a long time, didn't it? Next, you speeded things up by counting nickels first and then filling in the left over numbers with pennies. Shopping with dimes makes paying for things much faster! It helps to know how to count by 10's well, and it helps to know there are 10 dimes in a dollar.

Now, let's get some practice changing pennies and nickels for dimes. This time, your pennies will be in stacks of 10 and your nickels in stacks of two coins. Beside each stack of pennies, put a stack of two nickels and then add one dime.

You can quickly count how much money you have in all by simply counting the dimes. Say you have 7 stacks of coins. You would count: 10, 20, 30, 40, 50, 60, 70. You have 70¢ worth of dimes. This means you also have 70¢ worth of nickels, and another 70¢ worth of pennies. Now, let's take all that money and go shopping!

Shopping with dimes, pennies and nickels

Let's use the same toys we shopped for before. This time we will start with dimes and will be counting by 10's. The spinner is worth 99¢. Begin to count out dimes until you are very close, but not over the cost of the

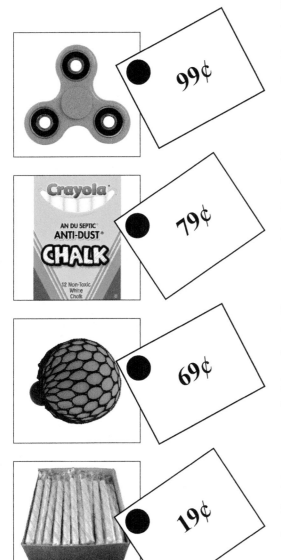

spinner. "10, 20, 30, 40, 50, 60, 70, 80, 90." We have to stop with the dimes! Can we use a nickel next? Yes! A nickel will bring us to 95¢. Now let's switch to pennies. "96, 97, 98, 99." You paid for the spinner using 9 dimes, 1 nickel, and 4 pennies.

The box of chalk costs 79¢. Start by counting dimes and remember to not go over the price of the chalk. "10, 20, 30, 40, 50, 60, 70." We are at 70¢ and need to get to 79¢. You can switch to nickels. If you add one nickel, you will be at 75¢. Now count out pennies: "76, 77, 78, 79." You used 7 dimes, 1 nickel, and 4 pennies.

The squishy ball costs 69¢. Can you just look at the price and guess how many dimes you will need? [Hint: look at the number on the left in 69¢]. 6 dimes, you say? You are right! Count them out: "10, 20, 30, 40, 50, 60." Now switch to nickels. One nickel brings you to 65¢. How many pennies will you need to reach the price? "66, 67, 68, 69." 4 pennies!

This last item should be super easy! Look at the price. 19¢. The left number sure makes it look like you need just one dime, doesn't it? And when prices end in a 9, we have learned that we will need one nickel and 4 pennies, right?

 Use Resource 3 to practice shopping with pennies, nickels, and dimes.

4 The Quarter

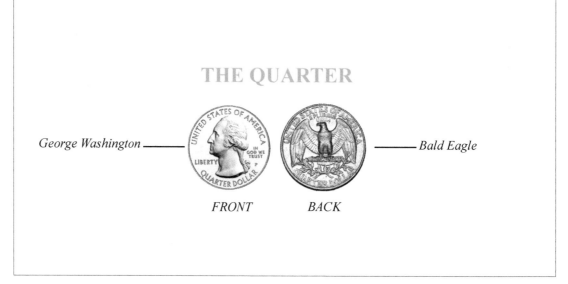

THE QUARTER

George Washington —— [coin front] —— [coin back] —— Bald Eagle

FRONT   BACK

About the Quarter

History

The first quarter was struck in 1796, but it wasn't produced regularly until 1831. When the USA was a very young country, England prohibited us from making our own money. So early Americans had to use currency from other countries. The most famous and widely-accepted currency was the Spanish Milled Dollar produced by Mexico and Peru since 1500! This coin was used in many parts of the world including our country.

The interesting thing about the Spanish Milled Dollar is that poeple used to cut it into 8 pieces in order to pay for less expensive things. Each section of the coin was worth 12 ½¢. If you had two of these "bits" of the Spanish Milled Dollar, you had what later became a quarter. Back in those days, people commonly talked about something costing "two bits."

The Washington quarter was not struck until 1932 to mark the 200th birthday of our first president, George Washington. The design was not meant to be permanent, but it ended up sticking around! The reverse of the quarter shows a bald eagle, the national bird.

In 1999, the US Mint began to create quarters that celebrated the each of the states. They called it the "America the Beautiful Quarters® Program. The design of each quarter celebrates something significant about the state it is showcasing. So far, not all the states are represented, but in 2018, five more states will have a commemorative quarter of their own!

RULE: One quarter is worth 25¢, which is also a quarter of a dollar.

This picture is pretty cool. It shows a quarter in the top, left corner, which is worth 25¢. Also you will see three other ways to show the value of a quarter.

1. A quarter is the same as 2 dimes and a nickel.
2. A quarter is the same as 5 nickels.
3. A quarter is the same as 25 pennies.

We know that there are 4 quarters in a dollar. If a dollar was divided into fourths, each fourth would be called a quarter. A quarter dollar. When we were studying time, we saw that the hour could be divided into fourths as well. Each quarter was 15 minutes. A fourth of a gallon is called a quart. Interesting stuff!

If you had 100 pennies, would you want to keep all of them, or would you want to trade some of them for other coins? What would you do? We have learned that when we are shopping we do need some pennies, but carrying 100 pennies around might not be convenient!

Let's play around with your coins and compare them to some prices. It will be fun, and it will make shopping and paying for things much easier!

Shopping with the Quarter

You are now armed with four kinds of coins. Let's shop for the same items as before, but this we will see if we can use a quarter or two...or even three!

The candy sticks cost 19¢. Can you use a quarter? [No. A quarter is worth 25¢ - more than the cost of the candy.] Can you use a dime? Look at the left number in the price. It is a 1 which means one dime. So, yes, you can use a dime. Can you use a nickel now? Yes! It will get you to 15¢. Now you can use 4 pennies to get to 19.

The squishy ball is 69¢. How many quarters can you start with as you pay for this? [Hint: look at

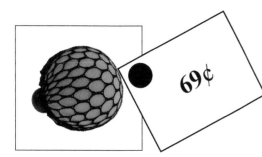

the left number. It is a 6. If two quarters = 50, you can use 2 quarters!] Now you are on the 50. How many dimes can you use? [Hint: one dime would get you to 60, Can you really use another one? No. It would take you over the price]. You already know how to pay for 9¢ with a nickel and 4 pennies.

The box of chalk costs 79¢. First let's figure out about how many quarters we can use to pay for the chalk. Let's see: 1 quarter is 25¢. 2 quarters would be 50¢ and 3 quarters would be 75¢! Wow! We are nearly to the price of the chalk. At this point, you can't use a nickel because it would take you to 80¢. So, count out the needed pennies: 76, 77, 78, 79.

The red spinner costs more than all the other items. Let's figure quarters first. Can you use the same procedure as you used for the chalk? You found that 3 quarters is 75¢. Can we add another quarter? No. That would take us to 100 and that is too much. So let's

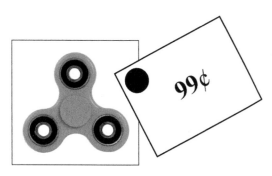

go back to the 75¢ we have reached by using 3 quarters. You can use dimes now. Count by 10s: 85, 95. and once again, we find you can't use a nickel! Count out pennies to reach 99¢. 96, 97, 98, 99.

The Many Ways to Make a Quarter

It is really fun to play with coins and experiment with different combinations of coins that can be used to reach the same target number.

For example, when you are shopping for the squishy ball, what if you look at your money and find you only have 1 quarter? We said we could use 2 quarters to start with. But if you don't have 2 quarters, does that mean you can't buy the squishy ball? Nope! Lay all your coins out and see how many different ways you can find to equal 69¢.

Here is another way to pay for the squishy ball. I look in my wallet and only have 1 quarter. So I lay that on the desk and start hunting for dimes. At this point, I have 25 + 10 + 10 for a total of 45¢. Now I will hunt for nickels. I find that I have 3 nickels. When I count my money now I have 25 + 10 + 10 + 5 + 5 + 5 for a total of 60¢. I will need to add 9 pennies to reach 69¢.

Let's count the money:

25, [switch to dimes] 35, 45, [switch to nickels] 50, 55, 60, [switch to pennies] 61, 62, 63, 64, 65, 66, 67, 68, 69.

Do you have another way of making 69¢? Let's see how many combinations of coins you can come up with!

RULE: A quarter is the same as 2 dimes + 1 nickel, or 5 nickels, or 25 pennies.

 Use Resource 4 to practice shopping with quarters, pennies, nickels, and dimes.

The Dollar

George Washington

FRONT

BACK

The Great Seal

About the Dollar

History

    The first dollar bill was printed in 1862 and by 1869, its design included a portrait of our first president, George Washington. George Washington played an active role in the birth of our country and so it was natural that he would be chosen to grace the dollar bill. All the symbolism on this bill has to do with gaining our freedom from Great Britain. On the back of the dollar bill is the Great Seal which shows a bald eagle, a symbol of our country. There are three places on the Great Seal that refer to the 13 colonies: the grouping of 13 stars above the eagles' head, the 13 stripes on the shield, and the 13 arrows the eagle grasps in this talon. In his other talon, he is clutching an olive branch containing 13 olives and 13 leaves. The arrows stand for war, while the olive branch stands for peace.

    On the left is an unfinished pyramid with 13 steps. Hovering above it is the eye of Providence, or God. Three Latin phrases speak to America's quest for independence from Britain. Novus Ordo Seclorum meaning "New order of the ages." No longer would America be under foreign rule. Annuit Coeptis means "He favors our undertaking." They believed they were on the side of right and that God was favoring their actions in rebelling against Britain. Finally, E Pluribus Unum means "Out of many [states], one [nation]."

What it buys

On this page is a picture showing what a dollar is worth.

There are 4 quarters in a dollar and we count them like this: 25, 50, 75, 100.

There are 10 dimes in a dollar and we count them like this: 10, 20, 30, 40, 50, 60, 70, 80, 90, 100.

There are 20 nickels in a dollar and we count them like this: 5, 10, 15, 20, 25, 30, 35, 40, 45, 50, 55, 60, 65, 70, 75, 80, 85, 90, 95, 100.

There are 100 pennies in a dollar and we count them like this: 1, 2, 3, 4, 5 and so on until we reach 100.

Sometimes it helps to see a whole "map" as we explore how we can make a 100. On the next page is a 5-frame of numbers to 100.

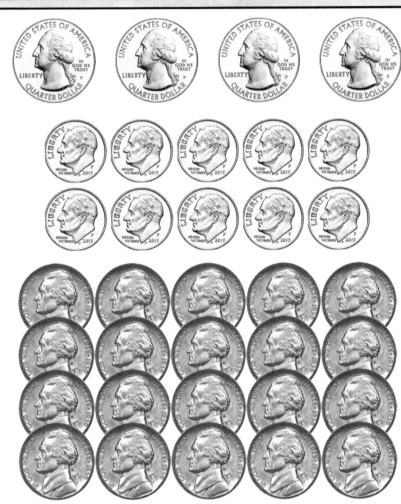

100 Pennies

Here is a five-frame of numbers 1-100. We are going to make friends with this chart because it will help us a lot as we become more and more comfortable with using money.

1	2	3	4	5
6	7	8	9	10
11	12	13	14	15
16	17	18	19	20
21	22	23	24	25
26	27	28	29	30
31	32	33	34	35
36	37	38	39	40
41	42	43	44	45
46	47	48	49	50
51	52	53	54	55
56	57	58	59	60
61	62	63	64	65
66	67	68	69	70
71	72	73	74	75
76	77	78	79	80
81	82	83	84	85
86	87	88	89	90
91	92	93	94	95
96	97	98	99	100

Let's study the chart. There are 100 spaces in all - the same number of pennies in a dollar.

Each row has 5 pennies, which is the same thing as a **nickel**! If you count by fives down the right hand column, you will quickly find that there are 20 nickels in a dollar.

Each two rows equals a **dime**. If you start on the 10 and count by 10's to 100, you will find you are skipping the number that end in a 5.

How many rows would equal a quarter? [Hint, you can count by fives or you can just look for the number 25 on the chart and count the rows.]

Try it out

What if you wanted to pay for something that costs 35¢? If you use the chart, you can look for the 35 and then figure out the coins you can use to pay.
• You could count out 35 pennies.
• You could use all nickels - 7 of them. Count by 5's down the column on the right to see if this is true.
• You could use dimes, too. But as you count by 10's down the right column, you will see you can't quite reach the 35 with just dimes. What coins can you use to get from 30 to 35? [5 pennies or a nickel].
• You could start with a quarter which would get you to the 25. You are still not quite at the 35 though. Can you use another quarter? [No. That would equal 50. Some options are to use a dime - that would equal 35¢. But you could also use two nickels or 10 pennies.]

Look for more shopping opportunities in a couple of pages.

Money and the 5-frame

Here is another view of coins on the 5-frame. Every single green number is a penny and there are 100 of them.

Since it takes 5 pennies to make a nickel and there are 5 pennies on each row, each row also represents a nickel. You can count the nickels in a dollar by just counting by 5's down the right column.

Dimes are exactly 2 rows or 2 nickels, or 10 pennies. No matter where you start on the chart, if you skip down exactly two rows, you will have added a dime. Try it. Put your finger on 47. To add a dime, just skip straight down two places. You will land on 57.

You can do something similar with the quarter. A quarter is 25 pennies or 5 nickels or 2 dimes and a nickel. It is also exactly 5 rows. Practice adding a quarter to any number on this chart. For example, find the 43 and add a quarter. Move straight down as you count 5 rows. "48, 53, 58, 63, 68."

Notice the patterns in the numbers. Column 1 ends in 1, 6, 1, 6, etc. Find the patterns in the other columns.

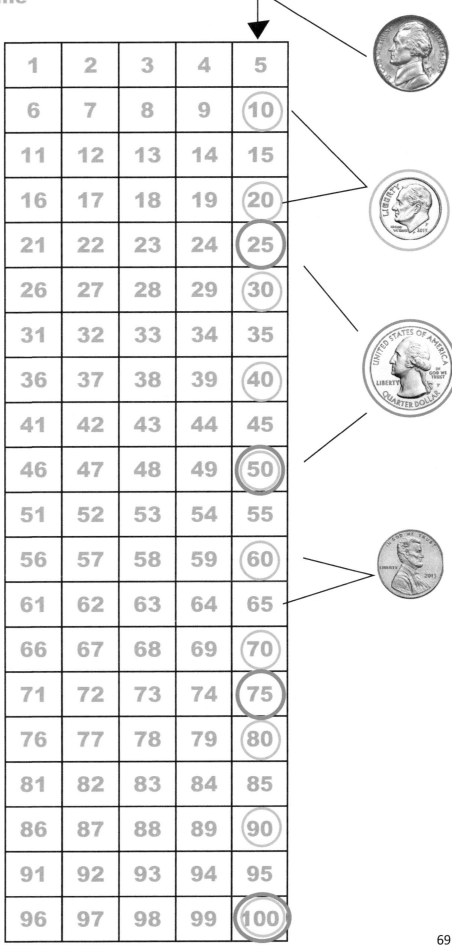

Shopping with Dollars

1	2	3	4	5
6	7	8	9	10
11	12	13	14	15
16	17	18	19	20
21	22	23	24	25
26	27	28	29	30
31	32	33	34	35
36	37	38	39	40
41	42	43	44	45
46	47	48	49	50
51	52	53	54	55
56	57	58	59	60
61	62	63	64	65
66	67	68	69	70
71	72	73	74	75
76	77	78	79	80
81	82	83	84	85
86	87	88	89	90
91	92	93	94	95
96	97	98	99	100

Up to this point, we have been using the ¢ sign because the items we have been "buying" cost less than a dollar. Now that we are shopping with dollars, we have to show prices differently.

When something costs more than a dollar, we write the prices like this: $1.25. The first sign is the dollar sign. The first number tells how many dollars. There is next a period that separates dollars from cents.

If something costs 4 dollars and 69¢, we would write the price like this: $4.69 without the ¢ sign.

Paying for items that cost more than a dollar is just as easy as paying for items that cost less than a dollar. You just look at the price and take out that many dollars, then figure the cents like you have been doing.

Hands-on practice

Let's practice counting out money. You will need some dollar bills and a good assortment of coins. Use the chart on the left if it helps you calculate the coins.

1. $2.17

2. $3.53

3. $1.29

4. $2.74

Feel free to show each price in different ways. For example the 17 cents in the first price can be

1 dime, 1 nickel and 2 pennies, OR

1 dime, 7 pennies, OR

2 nickels and 7 pennies, OR

3 nickels and 2 pennies.

Count out money to pay for these toys.

Colored pencils

$7.41 is the price. First count out the dollars, and then work on the cents. Show cents in at least two different ways.

[Hint. One easy way to show cents is 4 dimes and 1 penny.]

Figit Toy

$2.10 is the price. First count out the dollars, and then work on the cents. Show cents in at least two different ways.

[Hint: One easy way to show cents is 1 dime.]

UNO game

$4.68 is the price. First count out the dollars, and then work on the cents. Show cents in at least two different ways.

[Hint: One way to show cents is to reach 50 by using 2 quarters, reaching 60 by adding a dime, reaching 65 by using a nickel, and using 3 pennies to reach 68¢.]

RULE: One dollar is worth 4 quarters, 10 dimes, 20 nickels and 100 pennies.

Use Resource 5 to practice shopping with dollars and coins.

Paper Money

About Paper Currency

History

Before the civil war (1861 - 1865), currency in our country was made of silver or gold. When the war started, people were afraid and uncertain. They saw the prices of things they needed rising rapidly because of shortages, and they began to hoard their gold and silver coins. They did not want to spend their silver and gold for goods that were priced much higher than they were worth. This caused a problem because without spending their coins, they were not able to buy what they needed.

Congress authorized the United States Treasury to print paper money to pay for the war, and to take the place of the coins people were not willing to spend. The first paper notes printed were worth 1¢, 5¢, 25¢, and 50¢.

Bills currently being printed and circulated are shown on the right. The bills contain these images front and back:

- $1.00 - George Washington and the Great Seal
- $5.00 - Abraham Lincoln and the Lincoln Memorial
- $10.00 - Alexander Hamilton and the US Treasury
- $20.00 - Andrew Jackson and the White House
- $50.00 - Ulysses Grant and the US Capitol
- $100.00 - Benjamin Franklin and Independence Hall

Other bills that have been printed include the $2.00 bill (which is still printed but not used very often), and larger denominations such as the $500, $1,000, $5,000 and $10,000 bills. Those larger bills were no longer printed after 1946 because no one was using them.

Shopping with Paper Bills

When you are shopping and the prices climb higher, it is very useful to have bills greater than $1.00. Look at the items on this page. For this activity you will need some bills: at least 4 $1.00, one $5.00, and one $10.00. You will also need your coins.

The Stomp Rocket costs the most at $19.99. Let's count out the paper money first. Look at the number to the left of the decimal. It is 19. You will need to count out:

1. $10.00 - now we have $9.99 left
2. $5.00 - now we have $4.99 left
3. Four $1.00 - now we have all the dollars laid out.

Look at the 99¢ and begin to select coins starting with your largest coin. If you have three quarters, lay them out as you count, "25, 50, 75." That brings you to 75¢. If you have two dimes, lay them out as you count "85, 95." Now, you will definitely need four pennies. Count them out like this: "96, 97, 98, 99."

The Parachute costs $6.57. Which bill will you start with? If you start with $5.00, you will also need a $1.00. Now do the coins. To get to 50¢, use two quarters if you have them. To make 7¢ you may use a nickel and two pennies.

The Connect game costs $8.77. To make 8 dollars, you will use a $5.00 and three $1.00. For the coins, if you have three quarters, you will be almost there! Count them out: "25, 50, 75." Now add two pennies as you count: "76, 77."

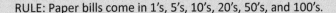

RULE: Paper bills come in 1's, 5's, 10's, 20's, 50's, and 100's.

Use Resource 6 to practice shopping with paper money and coins.

7 Adding Money

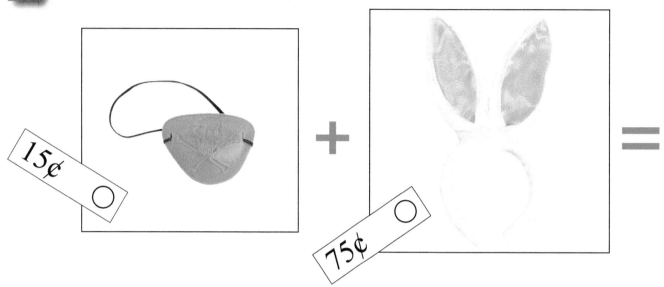

Why Add Money?

Most of the time when we go shopping, we don't just buy one thing. It is really important to know how to add the prices of two or more things. Say a girl named Lou wants to make a costume using pink things. Oh! Like the rabbit ears and the mask in the pictures above. If she is going to pay for them, she will need to add the two items and then make sure she has enough money to pay for them.

When you are adding two prices, look at the cents first. If you can tell the cents will be less than $1.00, adding the prices is pretty easy.

Add 15¢ and 75¢

Start with the 75 and count on. You can use 1 dime and 1 nickel, or you can use 3 nickels. Let's do it both ways. Say, "75, 85, 90." [3 quarters, 1 dime, 1 nickel]. Now say, "75, 80, 85." [3 quarters & 3 nickels].

If you have two prices and the cents are more than $1.00, you will need to put enough coins together to make a dollar first, then add what is left.

Add 75¢ and 50¢

Look at the coins first. If you have 75¢, that is three quarters. 50¢ is another two quarters. Can you make $1.00 with 5 quarters? Yes! And you will have a quarter left over. Write ".25" for the coins, then add 1 dollar for a total of $1.25.

Look at the prices below. One is $4.68 and the other $8.77. Use real coins to count or use scratch paper and draw the money. Use the approach that makes the most sense to you.

1. Look at the dollars first. There are 12 of them. Now, look at the cents.

77 is 3 quarters and 2 pennies. Count them: 25, 50, 75, 76, 77.

68 is 2 quarters and 1 dime, and 1 nickel and 3 pennies. 25, 50, 60, 65, 66, 67, 68.

Pick up 4 quarters ($1.00) and put it with the $12.00 you already set out. Now you have this left:

Let's count the money: 25, 35, 40, 41, 42, 43, 44, 45. OR if you notice that the 5 pennies = a nickel, you can count like this: 25, 35, 40, 45.

The two games cost $13.45. You will need a $10.00, three $1.00 bills, a quarter, and 2 dimes.

Let's look at this another way. This time if you want to quickly sketch the money, do that instead of counting out real money. You are going to add $4.68 and $8.77. Once again, take the dollars out. Set the 12 dollars to one side in your mind or draw them on your paper like this:

Now, let's see if we can make a dollar from the cents. Both amounts are more than 50¢, so it looks like we can make a dollar! First, take 50¢ from the 68, leaving 18 cents. Take 50¢ from the 77 leaving 27¢.

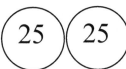

At this point you have $13.00 and you are going to add 18 and 27.

If you draw coins, they will look like this:

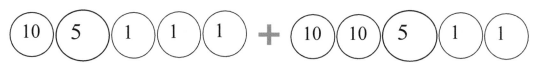

If you group the coins together that are alike, they will be easier to add:

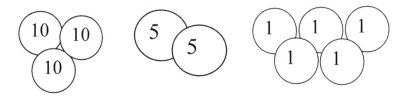

Let's count: 10, 20, 30, 35, 40, 41, 42, 43, 44, 45. OR you can see at a glance you have the equivalent of four dimes and another 5¢.

For those who like to just stack numbers up and add them, you can always make an addition problem from the two prices:

$$\begin{array}{r} \$4.68 \\ \underline{\$8.77} \end{array}$$

Use Resource 7 to practice shopping with dollars and coins.

Making Change

You pay $10.00...

for this...

and get back the "too much."

"$8.77.   78, 79, 80, 90, $9.00, $10.00"

Item + change = money paid.

Why Make Change?

In a magical world, every human on earth would be carrying a wallet with the exact amount of money in the exact value that they will need anytime they go shopping for anything ever. But we don't live in a *that kind* of a magical world! Usually we don't find that we have the right coins and bills in the exact amounts we need to pay for something. So we solve this by giving the shop keeper a bill larger than the cost of the item and the shop keeper gives us back the money we paid too much. We get the "too much" back! Shop keepers can do this because they have little drawers full of stacks of each kind of coin.

In the picture above, Oliver wanted to buy a Connect4 game that cost $8.77. He took a quick look in his wallet and saw only a $10.00. So he gave the shop keeper the $10.00 and the shop keeper gave him back the "too much" that he paid. This is what he did: He said the price of the game because that is what Oliver owed him, then as he counted out the coins above, he said, "78, 79, 80, [pennies] 90, $9.00 [dimes]" and then when he handed him the dollar bill, he finished with, "$10.00."

RULE: The item you pay for and the change you get must equal the money you paid.

Practice Making Change

Making change with bills.

On scratch paper, draw 3 big circles. In the first circle, write what you want to buy and how much it will cost. In the second circle, write the bill you will use to pay for the item. Remember that the bill needs to be larger in value than what your item costs. In the third circle, write your change. You can draw little circles for coins and rectangles for bills. Look at the picture to the right for a reminder.

What you want to buy and how much it costs:

A bill larger than the cost of the item.

This is for the "too much" that you will get back.

Here is another example of making change:

Anna wanted to buy an UNO game. The UNO game costs $4.68. Anna gave the shop keeper $5.00. The shop keeper will need to give Anna change. He will say the price of the game first: "$4.68. Then he will start with coins that will get him to the next big number. The shop keeper begins to count with pennies: "69,

70." He knows that if he can get to 70, he will be able to use bigger coins! Next he gives Anna a nickel and says, "75." He knew if he could reach 75, he would be able to use a quarter to get to the dollar mark Finally, he gives Anna a quarter as he says, "$5.00."

Play around with other circle trios. Sometimes you won't be using bills at all! What if you want to buy a candy stick for 19¢? If you give the shop keeper a quarter, you would need change back, right?

"$4.68... 69, 70, 75, $5.00."

78

Making change with bills and coins.

Let's do some shopping and pay with bills larger than a dollar. The red spinner is only 99¢. You don't have a $1.00, but you do have a $5.00! The shop keeper will say the price of your spinner, then will count your change, adding it to the price of your toy until he reaches the $5.00 you gave him.

What you buy: **what you pay:**   **what you get back:**

Say, "99. $1.00, 2.00, 3.00, 4.00, $5.00"

Say, "3.89. 3.90, 4.00, 5.00, and 5 is $10.00."

Say, "17.49. 50, 75, 18.00, 19.00, $20.00."

The bathtub toys cost $3.89. You could pay with a $5.00, but you already used it for the spinner. So you give the shop keeper $10.00. He will say the price of your toy: "$3.89." He will say, "90, $4.00," and as he gives you a dollar, he will say, "5.00 and 5 is $10.00," as he hands you a $5.00.

The construction toy costs $17.49. You pay with a $20.00. Shop keeper will say, "$17.49. 50, 75, 18.00," (as he switches to quarters) and then will finish by switching to dollar bills as he says, "19.00, $20.00."

Remember. When you count change, always watch for how to get to the a number that will let you switch to coins of higher value and then eventually to bills.

> RULE: In making change, say the price of the item, then start counting change to reach the amount paid.

   Use Resource 8 to practice making change.

Part II - Money Resources

In the pages following are resources for you to use with your child to practice working with money. One sheet may or may not be enough practice. If you feel your child needs more practice, use real objects and "play store."

For instance, in R-1 - Shopping with Pennies, there are 8 pictures of toys and candy with prices by them. When you have finished with this page, no need to look for another work sheet! Simply have your child find some objects to stock a store with. Little stickers on which to write prices would be perfect.

You may use play money if you wish, but giving your child real money to use will lend reality and relevance to the exercise.

R-1 - Shopping with Pennies

Let's go on a pretend shopping trip. Below are several items you might want to buy. Each item has a price in pennies. Decide which items you would like to purchase, and then add up the total number of pennies you will need to pay for everything you buy.

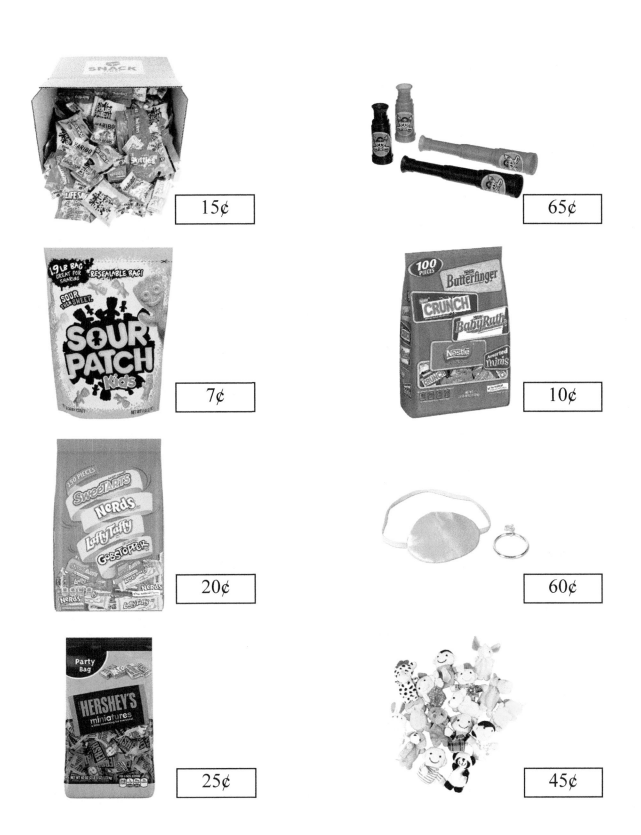

15¢

65¢

7¢

10¢

20¢

60¢

25¢

45¢

R-2 - Shopping with Pennies and Nickels

We found a garage sale selling games - all for under a dollar! Start with nickels first and count by 5's as you count out money to pay for each object. When you can no longer use nickels, finish the count with pennies, counting by 1's.

55¢

68¢

77¢

22¢

58¢

59¢

15¢

79¢

R-3 - Shopping with Pennies, Nickels, and Dimes

The garage sale also has some cool animal figures. Start with dimes first, then change to nickels and then use pennies to finish paying for your animals.

49¢

82¢

37¢

59¢

58¢

67¢

86¢

28¢

R-4 - Shopping with Pennies, Nickels, Dimes, and Quarters

Wow! You just found some cars from the Pixar movies! Count out money to pay for the cars, starting with quarters and then changing to dimes, nickels, and pennies as you need to.

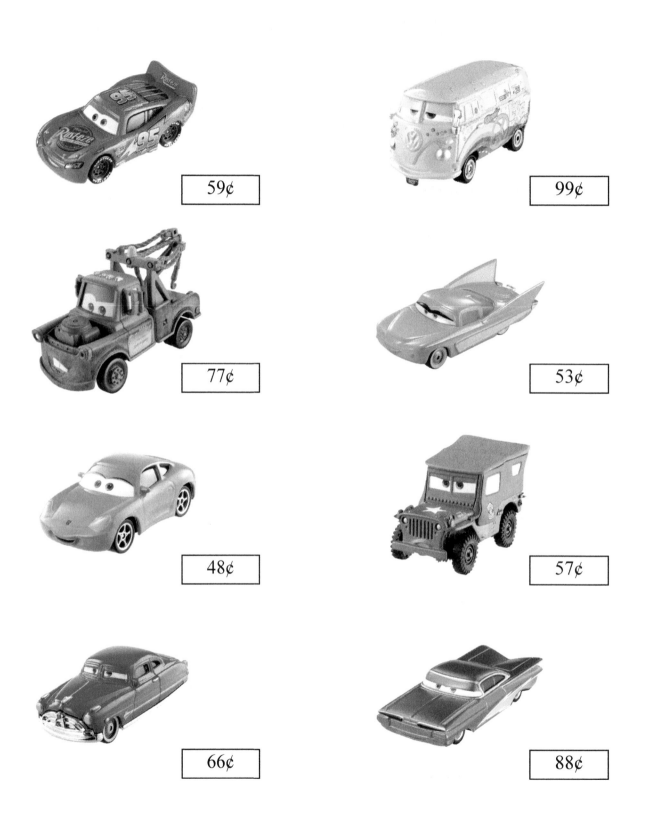

59¢

99¢

77¢

53¢

48¢

57¢

66¢

88¢

R-5 - Shopping with Dollars and Coins

Today you are shopping for water toys. This time, each toys costs at least one dollar. First, look at the number of dollars you will need, count them out, then count coins to finish paying.

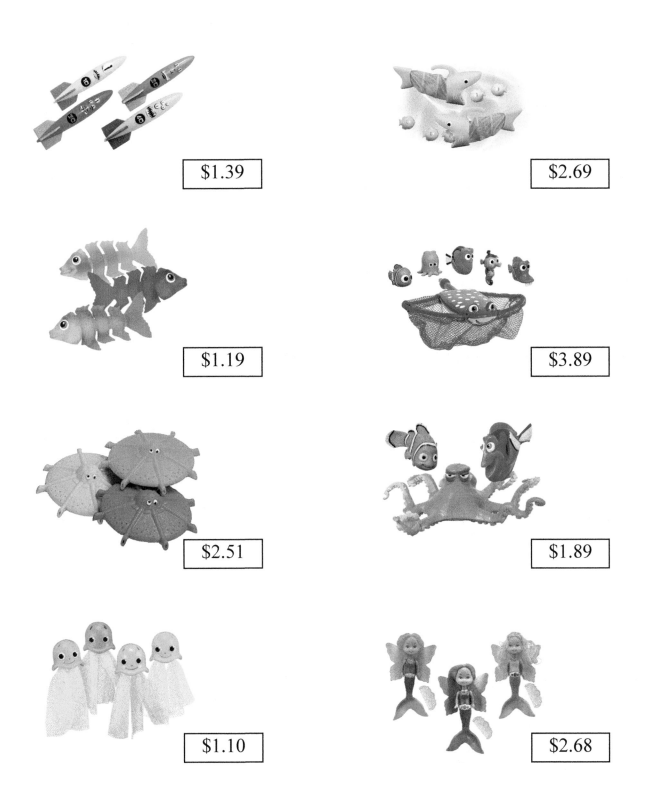

$1.39

$2.69

$1.19

$3.89

$2.51

$1.89

$1.10

$2.68

R-6 - Shopping with Bills and Coins

Today you are shopping for building sets. First, look at the number of dollars you will need, count them out, then count coins to finish paying.

$11.36

$12.58

$10.29

$17.49

$15.57

$8.29

$13.97

$6.79

Right-Brained Time, Money, & Measurement © 2017 Sarah Major, Child1st Publications, www.child1st.com.

R-7 - Adding Money

Today you get to choose two things to buy... four times! FIrst, draw lines connecting pairs of items. The first one is done for you. Next, add the money you will need to pay for each pair of items.

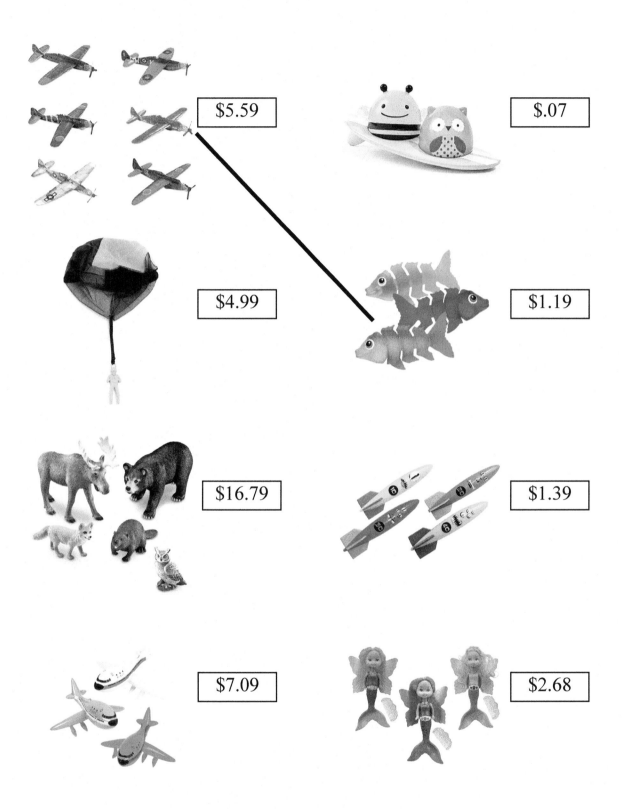

$5.59

$.07

$4.99

$1.19

$16.79

$1.39

$7.09

$2.68

R-8 - Making Change

Today you will be paying with bills. The bill you choose to pay with will be worth more than the cost of the item you are buying. First, look at the price of the toy. Next, write the number on the bill that matches the bill you will be paying. Finally, count out change by saying the price of the item, then using pennies to get to the next 10. When you have finished counting out the change, draw your coins to the right of the item you bought. The cost of the item plus the change you got should equal the bill you paid.

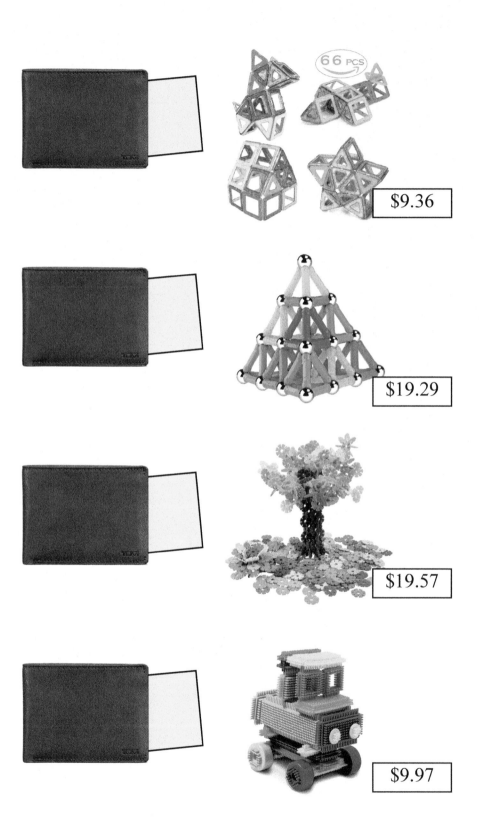

66 PCS

$9.36

$19.29

$19.57

$9.97

Right-Brained Time, Money, & Measurement © 2017 Sarah Major, Child1st Publications, www.child1st.com.

R-8 - Making Change

Today you will be paying with bills. The bill you choose to pay with will be worth more than the cost of the item you are buying. First, look at the price of the toy. Next, write the number on the bill that matches the bill you will be paying. Finally, count out change by saying the price of the item, then using pennies to get to the next 10. When you have finished counting out the change, draw your money to the right of the item you bought. The cost of the item plus the change you got should equal the bill you paid.

$14.95

$17.09

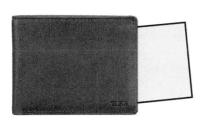 

$9.69

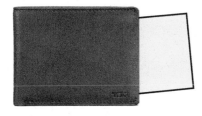 

$7.46

Part III - Measurement

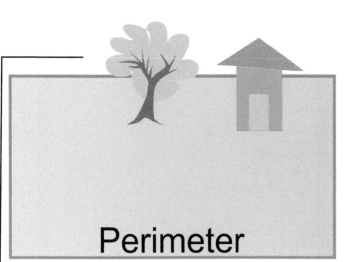

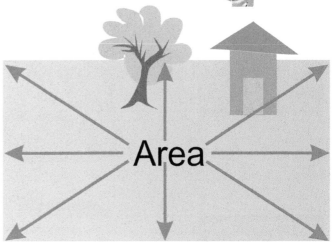

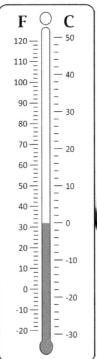

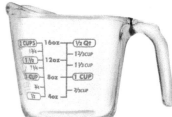

1 Temperature

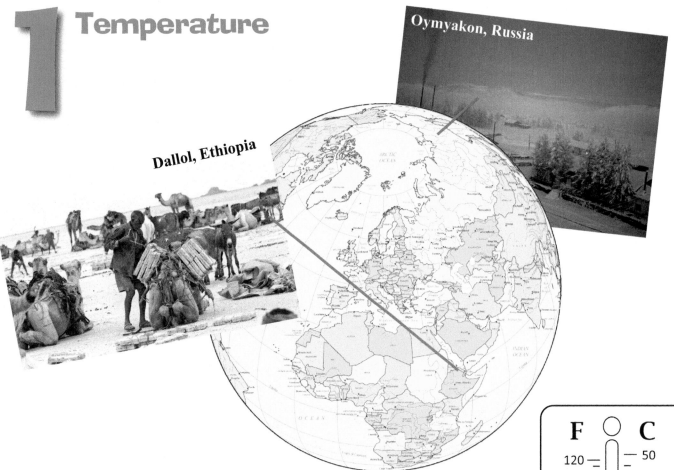

Dallol, Ethiopia

Oymyakon, Russia

All Kinds of Weather

One of the most important things we measure is the weather. We check the temperature nearly every day so we know how to dress. The weather can be extreme in some places in the world. Dallol, Ethiopia is the hottest inhabited place on earth with a record temperature of 125° recorded. One of the coldest inhabited places on earth is Oymyakon, Russia which was -90° in 1933. Those temperatures, both hottest and coldest, are extremes! Normally, outdoor temperatures can be measured by a regular thermometer.

Thermometers measure air temperature

Look at the thermometer on the right. The left columnn of numbers has a big F and has numbers starting at -20 and rising to 120 degrees. The F stands for Fahrenheit. Gabriel Daniel Fahrenheit was a German physicist who invented the mercury thermometer to measure air temperature clear back in 1714! On the right is a column of numbers under a C. That C stands for Celsius. This way of measuring temperature was invented by a Swedish astronomer called Anders Celsius. Many countries in the world use the Celsius temperature scale for measuring air temperature.

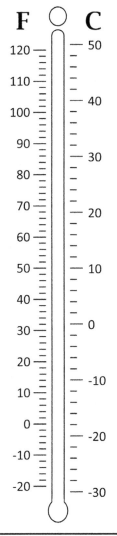

A thermometer measures the temperature of the air around it. Many thermometers have a glass tube that contains mercury or alcohol. If the air around the glass tube begins to heat up, the liquid inside the tube also heats up and expands. When this happens, the liquid moves up the glass and shows us the temperature of the air.

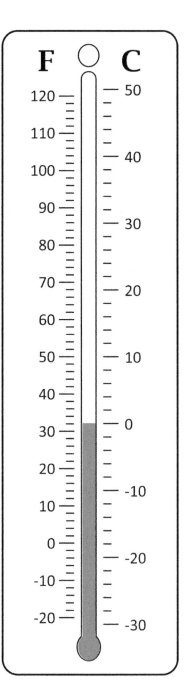

Freezing and boiling water

On a Fahreheit scale, when water temperature cools to 32°, it will freeze. If the water is heated, once it reaches 212°, it will boil. On a Celsius scale, water freezes at 0° and boils at 100°. The thermometer on the right shows a temperature of 32° F. and 0° C: the temperature at which water freezes. You will notice that there is no mark on this thermometer for the point at which water boils! We need a different kind of thermometer to measure boiling water.

Cooking temperatures

There are many times people like to measure the temperatures of liquids and foods as they heat up. We use a different kind of thermometer for this purpose. This thermometer has a dial with numbers. Notice that the numbers begin at 0° and go up to 220° and that the pointed end is stuck into the turkey. This thermometer will measure boiling liquid or food for sure, since the numbers go up to 220°.

Measuring body temperature

When you get sick and get a fever, your parents or the doctor will take your temperature to see just how sick you are. This requires yet another thermometer. Normal body temperature is about 98.6° so the thermometer needs to show not only the degrees, but fractions of degrees as well. Here is a body thermometer showing the red liquid that rises up the glass tube to mark the person's body temperature.

Notice that on the thermometers, some of the lines have numbers by them. They have little lines without numbers in between - just like a clock does.

On a clock, the little lines with no numbers represent minutes. On thermometers, the little lines show degrees of heat.

- Sometimes you will be counting by 10's like on the weather thermometer.
- The food thermometer counts by 20's, but the little lines between the numbers let you count by 2's.
- Body thermometers count by 1's but have little lines between them that represent tenths of degrees! When a person's temperature is 98.6° it means their temperature is 98 degrees and 6 tenths of a degree more.

Practice reading temperatures

You will need the three different types of thermometers we have talked about.

Temperature of the air

For a week or two, read an outdoor thermometer each day at the same time and record the temperature on a sheet of blank thermometers. (See the Measurement Resources section for blank thermometers.)

Temperature of food and liquids

Using a food thermometer, measure and record the temperature on another sheet from Measurement Resources. Ideas of foods to measure include: boiling water, chicken from the oven, a baked casserole, meat on the grill, and taffy (or other candy) cooking.

Body temperature

Get 3-5 volunteers and take their temperatures. Record them on a sheet (see Measurement Resources). Not every person has exactly the same temperature! Your family might have a digital thermometer that shows the temperature in numbers like this:

RULE: Use thermometers to measure temperature. "Thermos" & "metron" mean "heat measure." in Greek.

Use Resource 1 to practice measuring temperature.

Length

Why Measure Length?

People have been measuring things since ancient times - about 300 years Before Christ, or B.C. The oldest known measurements of length were in Egypt. The main unit of measurement was the cubit. A cubit is the distance from the tip of your middle finger to your elbow. They next broke the cubit down into half cubits which were called spans and were measured by spreading out their hands and measuring from the very tip of their little finger to the tip of their thumb. Here are some examples of ancient measurements:

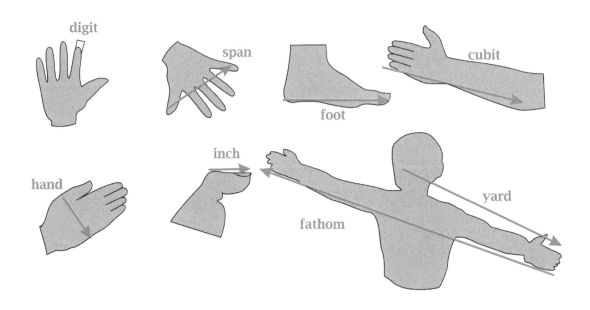

Look at the men on the left. If they are going to measure a cubit, do you think the cubits they measure will be the same? How about if they measure a span? Do you see the problem?

Here's an original fable that explains why people started feeling it was important to have a way to measure things fairly.

Farming in Farmville

The town was Farmville and the farmers in Farmville all raised inch worms. Yes, it is true. Inch worms. Each farm in Farmville was supposed to be the same size. The farmers had a meeting and agreed that they would measure the length of each side of their square farms by walking toe to toe as they counted how many feet their farm measured. They agreed that each side should measure three feet. This would create a nice, square yard for their worms to enjoy.

Everything was fine until a new farmer came into town and decided to start his own worm farm. He carefully paced out his farm and built his fences. The other farmers watched carefully. Why? Because this new farmer was very, very tall and his feet were very, very long. What happened is that his farm was much bigger than everyone else's farm. Everyone started noticing that farms weren't really all the same size like they thought they were.

At the next village meeting there was a lot of loud discussion. Lots of ideas were thrown around. One idea was to choose one man to pace and measure every farm. This man was not happy. He thought he would be spending all his time measuring instead of raising worms. Another idea they came up with was using foot long hot dogs to measure with. Great idea right? Only problem is that they rotted and stunk horribly!

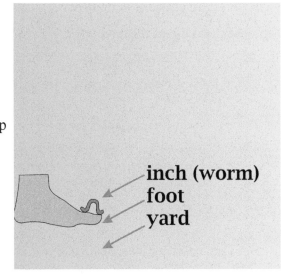

inch (worm)
foot
yard

One small boy watched and listened. At last he walked to the front of the room and held up his hand. In it he had a wooden foot he had carved while everyone was discussing. He suggested that each farmer use the wooden foot to measure their farms. This way each yard would be the same. The farmers were ecstatic and they all got back to work!

Units of Length
Inch

Because of Farmville, we know that inch worms are about an inch long. They are interesting creatures that have legs only in the front and back of their body. When they walk, they hump up and then stretch out, looking very much like they are measuring length. Right under the inchworm is a rectangle that shows the size of an inch.

inchworm

1 inch

Foot

Also because of Farmville, we know a foot is about the length of a man's foot. Here is a picture of a man's foot with a ruler lying beside it. This foot happens to be a foot long! We can't show the foot and ruler exactly a foot long because it would not fit into this book. This ruler is 12 inches long and 12 inches = a foot!

A great thing you can do is grab a ruler and then find some adults and measure their feet. The foot closest to the length of the 12 inch ruler wins!

If you keep a record of the feet you measure, you can also record

the number of inches long each foot is. You will measure each foot by lining up the zero to the back of their heel, then look at where their toe ends. If the toe doesn't land exactly on a number, look at the ruler below:

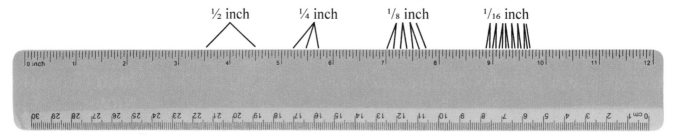

Between each number are little lines. Identify the lines that are exactly halfway between the numbers. These are half inch lines. Also between inches are three lines that mark quarter inches. Next we see lines that mark eighth inches, and finally sixteenth inches.

When you are measuring feet, it is enough to record a person's foot measurement as so many inches and a half, if their toes pass one number but don't quite reach the next number. My own foot, for example, is 9 inches a bit more, so I can say, "My foot is about 9½ inches long." This is how I would write it: 9½".

Yard

Remember from Farmville that each of the inchworm farms were a yard (or three feet) on a side? We are going to look at a yardstick - a great way to measure three feet at one time. A yardstick is a lot like a 12" ruler except it has the equivalent of three 12" rulers end to end. A yardstick measures 3 x 12 or 36 inches.

One item that is usually measured in yards is cloth or fabric. People who sew get used to

measuring by the yard, by the half yard (18"), and by the quarter yard (9").

Maybe the pattern calls for 2½ yards. The shop keeper will measure two lengths that are the length of the yardstick, then will measure 18" more. This will make 2½ yards.

Many feet

Sometimes what we need to measure would be hard to measure using a yardstick or a ruler. What if you had a long fence around your back yard and you wanted to measure quickly? You could use a tape measure. Tape measures are pretty cool! They hold a very long metal tape rolled up inside a case that is actually quite small.

When you measure with a tape measure, you can ask someone to hold the zero end of the tape

measure at the beginning of the fence, then you can walk away towards the end of the fence, letting the tape pull out. When you reach the end of the fence, look at the tape measure and notice which number is by the end of the fence.

This is how long your fence is.

Practice Measuring

This is the fun part! You are going to get to go all over your house and yard and find things to measure. Small things can be measured with a ruler. Larger things can be measured with a yardstick, while really long things can be measured with a measuring tape.

Your list may look like this:

Mailbox: _____inches

Birdfeeder: _____inches

Window: _____feet.

Front porch: _____ yards

INCHES:

You can either write 5 inches, or 5 in., or 5".

FEET:

You can either write 5 feet, or 5ft., or 5'.

YARDS:

You can either write 5 yards, or 5 yds.

Important:

When you start to measure, make sure the zero line is even with one end of the object you are measuring.

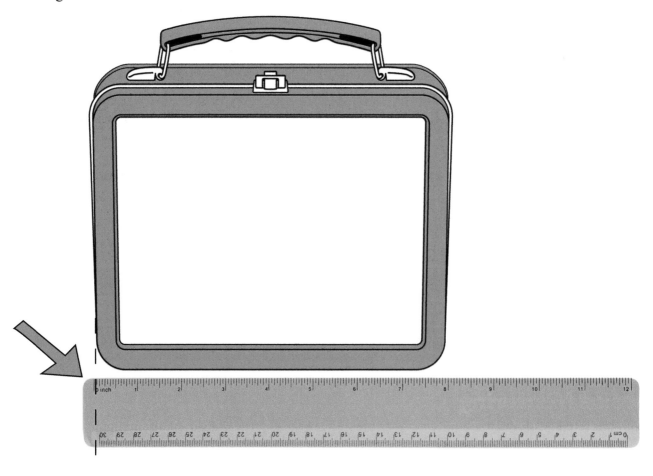

RULE: We measure inches, feet, yards with rulers, yardsticks, and tape measures.

 Use Resource 2 to practice measuring length.

3 Perimeter

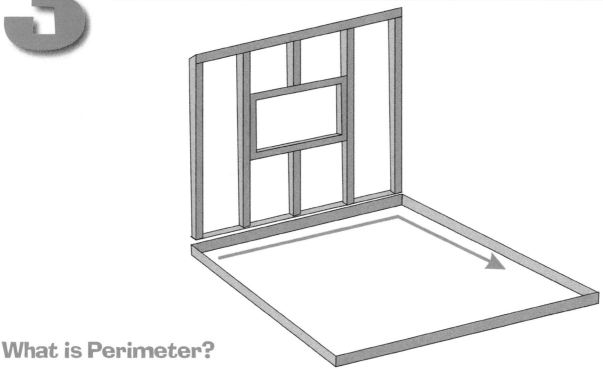

What is Perimeter?

Just like it is useful to know how long something is, it is very important to know the perimeter of an object or area. Perimeter is a word that has its roots in the Greek language. "Peri" means "around" in Greek while "metros" means "measure." Perimeter, then, means the measure around a shape. Look at the tree house frame in the picture above. The red arrow shows the boards that make up the perimeter of the floor.

If you are building a treehouse, you start by making a platform. What holds the floor is a frame made of wood. You must know the perimeter of the floor you want in order to buy the right boards to make a frame.

Let's do an example together. Find a yardstick or a tape measure and go find a coffee table. You will also need a pencil and some scratch paper. First, measure a side and write down the measurement. Say the first side of the table is 4 feet. Next, measure the second side. Say that side measures 2 feet. Continue by measuring each side and writing down the measurements. When you have finished, you will have four numbers. To find how many feet around the edge of the table, you will need to add all four numbers together. What you will have is 4' + 2' + 4' + 2' = 12'. Try another smallish object - a small rug or the window of the oven on the stove. Write the four measurements down and then add them up.

Do you notice a pattern? [Hint: two of the sides are always the same and the other two are always the same.] Does this suggest a shortcut? I think so! You can measure a long side, a short side, add them together, and double the number. For instance, the coffee table: 4' + 2' is 6'. Double of 6' is 12'. The only time this shortcut works is with squares or rectangles.

Measuring squares and rectangles

We found when we were learning to find the measure of a perimeter that we can measure only two sides and then double their sum to find the perimeter. Let's look at some smaller examples now. Decide what measuring tool you want to use to measure these.

Find a book, a box of cereal or pasta, an envelope, a pot holder, a game box, and a set of cards. On scratch paper, write the name of each of the things you will be measuring. Make sure to measure a long side and a short side, add them together, then double them.

Measuring Irregular Shapes

Sometimes we will need to measure perimeters of shapes that are not square or rectangular. Maybe you need to know the perimeter of a triangle. In this case, you will measure all three sides, then you will add the measurements to reach the perimeter.

With a ruler and graph paper, draw some shapes.* Here is an example:

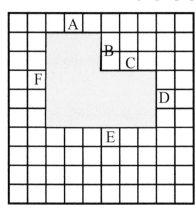

You can find perimeter using graph paper by just counting the number of squares on each side of the shape. This shape has 6 sides. Let's start on the top and go to the right, writing the measurements for each side.

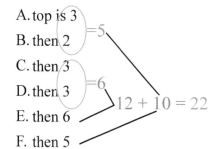

A. top is 3
B. then 2
C. then 3
D. then 3
E. then 6
F. then 5

=5
=6
12 + 10 = 22

Add the sides together: 3+2+3+3+6+5 = 22. The perimeter is 22 squares. [A shortcut for adding those numbers: A. make a 5 from the 3+2 B. add it to the other 5 to get 10. C. add 3+3 to get 6 then add to the other 6 to get 12. D. Now add 10 + 12 to get 22.]

*Keep your graph paper shapes for use in the next chapter on area.

RULE: We find perimeter by adding the measurements of all sides together.

Use Resource 3 to practice measuring perimeter.

4 Area

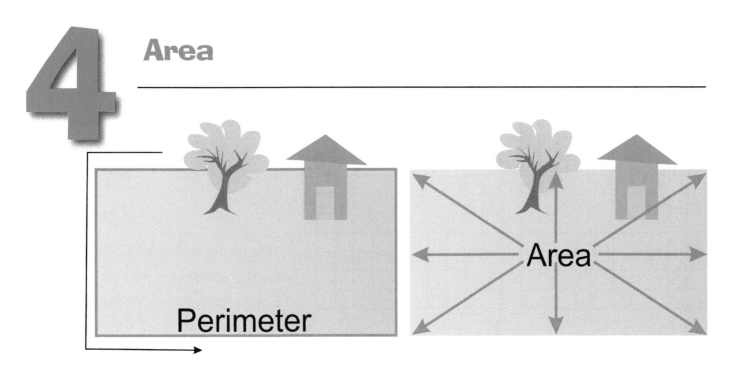

What is Area?

Area is a very different thing from perimeter, but both are very useful! The word area refers to how much space is within a certain boundary. The left picture, above, shows a red fenceline which goes around the perimeter of the property. The second picture shows area, or how much actual space is on the property. Picture "area" as being everything that is covered by grass. When you buy carpet for your living room, you need to figure area. And best of all, when you are building a tree house, you need to figure out the area of the floor so you will know how much flooring you will need.

Measuring Area

Measuring area can be easy and fun. Let's say in building a fort we think that 12" tiles would be perfect for the floor. We need to calculate how many tiles we will need. First we will measure the floor. We find the floor is exactly 10' by 10'. This means each side measures 10 feet. We can see on the picture that the floor has been marked to show where each tile will lay. What will be the easiest way to figure out how many tiles we will need?

1. Count each tile. This is the slow way!

2. Calculate: if there are 10 rows of 10 tiles, couldn't we just multiply 10 (rows) X 10 (tiles)? Yes! 10 X 10 = 100. We need 100 tiles!

On a side note. What is the perimeter of this floor? It will be useful to have this information when it comes time to make baseboards. Since each side is the same, we can do 4' X 10' = 40'.

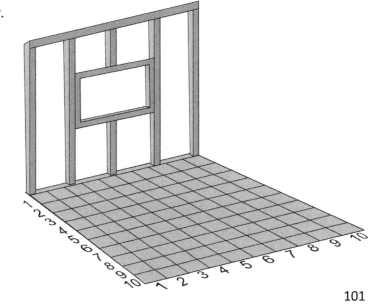

Measuring Area for Irregular Shapes

Sometimes we need to know the area for shapes that are not square or rectangular. Maybe your treehouse has a bump out. The floor plan for the tree house would now look like the drawing below. This

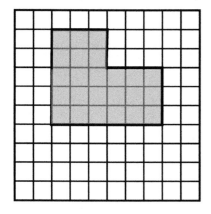 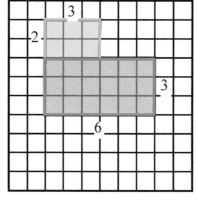

shape is irregular, but it is made up of two rectangles, isn't it? So we can figure the area of the two rectangles and add them together.

The orange rectangle is 2' on the short side and 3' on the long side. 2 X 3 = 6. The green rectangle is 3' on the short side and 6' on the long side. 3 X 6 = 18'. Now, in order to get the area for the whole shape we just need to add the two areas together. 6 + 18 = 24. The area of this tree house floor is 24.

Practice Measuring Area

This will be fun! Find some objects that have a flat surface. You can use some of the same object you found before, or you can hunt for new ideas. You can measure the area of a rug, a dining table, a piece of drawing paper, a closet floor, a deck, the floor of a birdfeeder, etc.

For each object you measure, decide if you are going to measure inches or feet. Write the name of the objects you chose on a sheet of paper and then gather your measuring tools: ruler, yardstick, and tape measure.

How to write measurements of area:

When we measure area, we need to use the word "square." Instead of just inches or feet, we say "square inches," or "square feet." This is because area is not a line like a fence or a wall. It is a flat space like a tile or a yard with grass.

INCHES:

You would say, "The area of the book is 56 square inches."

FEET:

You would say, "The rug is 18 square feet."

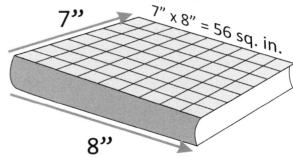

RULE: We find area by measuring two sides and multiplying them.

Use Resource 4 to practice measuring area.

5 Weight

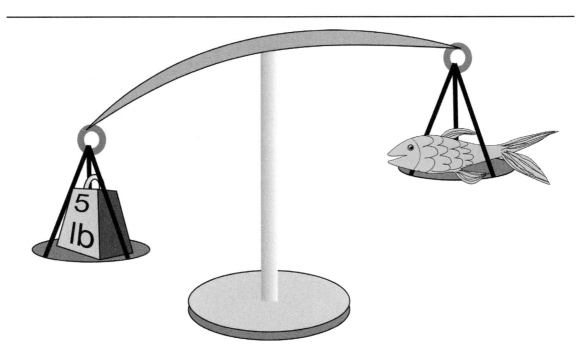

What is Weight?

When we talk about what something weighs, we are talking about how heavy it is. Say you find two baseball bats and pick one up in each hand, then you notice that one feels a lot heavier than the other. Or maybe you go bowling. You lift each ball until you find one that works for you without being too heavy to lift and throw. How heavy something is really does matter!

We measure weights using scales of various kinds. Here are some examples. In the top picture, a scale is comparing the weight of a fish to a five pound weight. Because the 5-pound weight is lower than the fish, we know it is heavier than the fish.

To the right is a scale that measures pounds and ounces. We see from this scale that the fish actually weighs about 4½ pounds because the arm is pointing between the 4 and the 5.

In the bottom picture, a HUGE fish is on a bathroom scale that people use to weigh themselves. Apparently this fish was far too heavy to be weighed on the balance scale or the 5 pound scale!

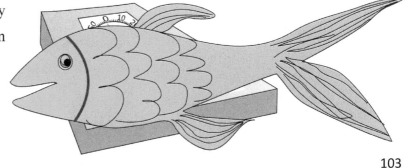

There are many machines that measure weight, but for now, let's look at how we talk about weight.

Measuring Weight

Generally when we talk about weight, we talk about pounds and ounces. Here is a picture of a kitchen scale. Notice the large numbers, which mark the pounds. There are slightly shorter lines between each pound, which mark half pounds.

There are 16 ounces in each pound. Each little short line represents 2 ounces. If one pound is 16 ounces, then ½ a pound is 8 ounces.

In the yellow scale on the right, notice the red needle. It has passed the 1 and is half way to the 2. This scale shows that the item weighs 1½ pounds.

Let's gather some items from around the house or classroom and weigh them so we can become familiar with how heavy each item is.

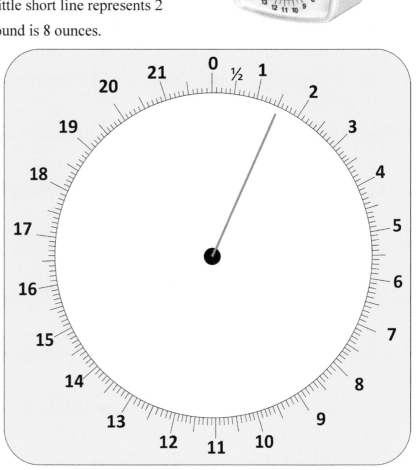

Weighing in the kitchen:

For this activity you will need a kitchen scale and some items - some light and some heavier. For example, you could find a pencil, a book, a magazine, a box of colored pencils, a pencil box, etc. List the items you found and as you weigh each one, write the weight beside the item.

The kitchen pantry is a good place to find items to weigh. Many of the boxes and cans already have their weight written on the packaging. Notice that the weight is written like this: NET WT 8 OZ. This means "Net weight, 8 ounces." Net weight is how much the food actually weighs without its packaging.

Practice finding weight on a scale, using the blank face just below. The first picture on the previous page says 8 OZ. Draw a light pencil line on the scale face showing where 8 OZ is. Next, the blue and brown bag of coffee says 20 OZ. Hmmm. That bag weighs more than a pound because we know one pound is 16 ounces. Find the 1 mark and say, "16 ounces." Count to 20 from there as you touch each little short mark: "18, 20." This bag of coffee is 20 ounces which is the same as 1 pound and 4 ounces. The last picture says 32 OZ. If you add 16 + 16, you will find it is 32. So 32 ounces is the same as 2 pounds.

When you write ounces you abbreviate like this: OZ. When you write pounds, you abbreviate like this: LB. "Pound" in Latin is "libra, and it is the Latin word that is being abbreviated.

Now look at the pictures below. These weights show pounds.

The first one says NET WT 20 OUNCES. (1 LB. 4 OZ). One pound is 16 ounces, and the extra 4 ounces is the same as a fourth of a pound. They could have written the weight like this: NET WT 1¼ LBS.

The last picture says 40 OZ. We know that 32 ounces is the same as 2 pounds. The extra 8 ounces makes ½ of a pound. Draw a pencil line on the scale face showing where these two weights fall.

Weighing People

It would be fun to do this section of measuring weight with some friends. What you need is a bathroom scale and some other kids. Most bathroom scales today don't look like this one, but I like it because it has a huge dial. You and all your friends could use this scale to weigh yourselves because it will weigh a person that weighs 350 pounds!

One a piece of paper, write your name and each of your friends' names. Weigh each person, writing their weight by their name. You will write their weight like this: Tommy - 62 LBS. Lbs means "pounds."

Your scale might be digital. If so, the weight will be super easy to write. All you have to do is copy what you see on the scale. The person who stood on this digital scale weighs 98.5 LBS, or 98½ pounds.

Weighing Heavy Things

If you want to weigh something very heavy... say an African elephant... you might want to talk about how many TONS the elephant weighs. A ton is the same as 2,000 pounds!

Look at the pictures below. The car weighs about 2 tons, while the elephant weighs about 7 tons. How many pounds does each weigh? The car is 2 tons or 2 x 2,000 pounds, or 4,000 LBS. The elephant weighs 7 x 2,000 or 14,000 LBS. Just for fun, look at the weights of you and your friends. How many of you would it take to weigh as much as the elephant?

Mass and Weight

Mass

We normally talk about how much something or someone *weighs*. Technically, we should talk about someone or something's *mass*. Mass means how much matter is in the object or person. For example, the mass of a bag of cotton is small compared to the mass of a bag of rocks of the same size. We talk about the mass of something saying pounds, ounces, or tons. But how much that object weighs depends on where it is.

Weight

Weight refers to how much force an object or a person exerts on the earth as a result of gravity. An elephant with a mass of 7 tons pushes on the earth with the force of 7 tons because of gravity pulling it down. But what if you loaded the elephant into a rocket ship and took him to the moon? Would the elephant (who's mass is still 7 tons) weigh 7 tons on the moon? No! The elephant would only weigh a little over 2 tons on the moon. And what if, on the way to the moon, the rocket ship burst open and the elephant floated out into space? The elephant, with its mass of 7 tons, would weigh nothing because in space, all matter is weightless. There is no gravity at work in space. Mass never changes unless the object changes, but weight can change depending on where it is.

RULE: We use "ounces, pounds, and tons" when we speak of weight.

 Use Resource 5 to practice measuring weight.

6 Volume

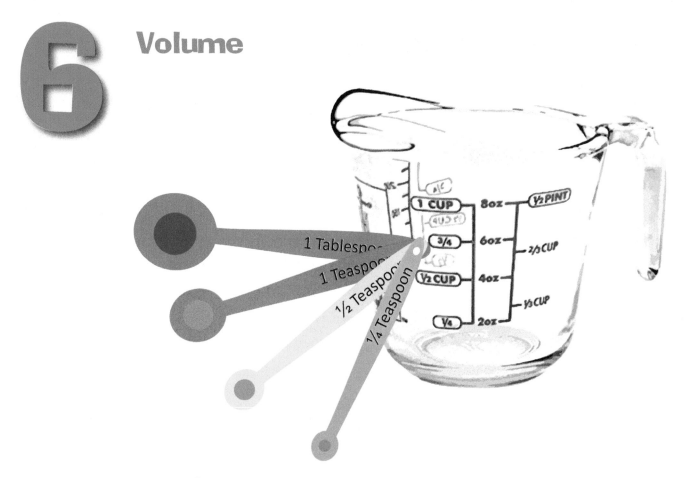

What is Volume?

When we speak of the volume of an object, what we mean is how much space it takes up. Volume is very different from mass (and different from weight). Mass tells us how dense something is while volume tells us how much room it takes up.

Let's try an experiment. Find two cups that are exactly the same size and the same weight. You can use two plastic tumblers or two paper cups. Now, fill one with dirt or sand. Fill the other one with leaves or grass pressed together. Fill both cups equally full. Now, using a kitchen scale, weigh each cup. Which cup has more mass? Which is heavier? This experiment proves that while two things might take up the same amount of space (they are the same volume) they aren't necessarily the same mass or weight.

Which could you lift: a laundry basket full of rocks or the same laundry basket full of cotton balls? ? The volume of each is the same because you are using the same laundry basket each time. But one has far more mass and is far heavier.

I. Measuring the Volume of Liquid

The tools we use to measure the volume of liquid include measuring spoons, measuring cups, pints, quarts, and gallons. The chart on the next page is a handy way to compare the volume of each. Also look at the spoons at the top of this page: There are 1 tablespoon, 1 teaspoon, ½ teaspoon, and ¼ teaspoon.

One gallon = 4 quarts, or 8 pints, or 16 cups, or 128 ounces.

One quart = 2 pints, 4 cups, or 32 ounces.

One pint = 2 cups or 16 ounces.

One cup = 8 ounces.

One ounce = 2 tablespoons.

1 tablespoon = 3 teaspoons.

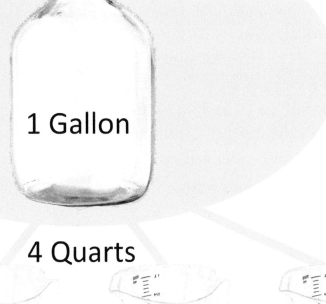

1 Gallon

4 Quarts

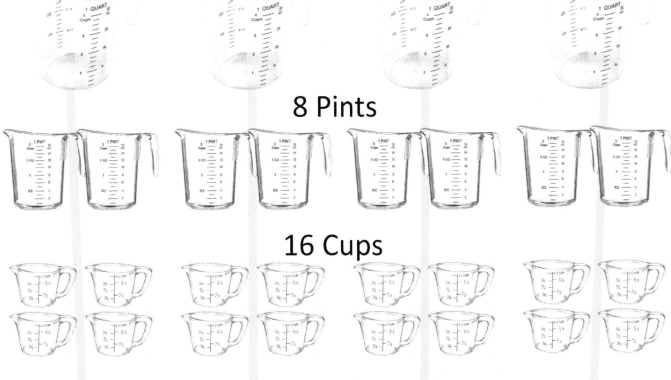

8 Pints

16 Cups

RULE: We measure liquid volume using spoons, ounces, cups, pints, quarts, and gallons.

Practice Measuring With Cups and Spoons

The very best way to practice measuring is by actually making something you will enjoy making! Gather your tools. You will need a measuring cup, measuring spoons, a large bowl, cookie sheets, spatula, and the ingredients listed below. When you measure, make sure the item is right at the top of each spoon, or that it comes right up to the correct line on the measuring cup. Arrows are pointing to measures you will use.

King Arthur Chocolate Chip Cookies

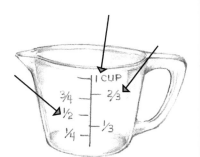

2/3 cup light brown sugar, firmly packed

2/3 cup granulated sugar

1/2 cup unsalted butter, right from the fridge, or at room temperature

1/2 cup vegetable shortening

3/4 teaspoon salt (use 1/2 teaspoon salt if you use salted butter)

2 teaspoons vanilla extract

1/4 teaspoon almond extract, optional

1 teaspoon vinegar, cider or white

1 teaspoon baking soda

1 large egg

2 cups King Arthur Unbleached All-Purpose Flour

2 cups semisweet chocolate chips

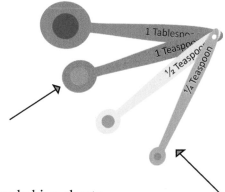

Directions

• Preheat the oven to 375°F. Lightly grease (or line with parchment) two baking sheets.

• In a large bowl, combine the sugars, butter, shortening, salt, vanilla and almond extracts, vinegar, and baking soda, beating until smooth and creamy.

• Beat in the egg, again beating till smooth. Scrape the bottom and sides of the bowl with a spatula to make sure everything is thoroughly combined.

• Mix in the flour, then the chips.

• Use a spoon (or a tablespoon cookie scoop) to scoop 1 1/4" balls of dough onto the prepared baking sheets, leaving 2" between them on all sides; they'll spread.

• Bake the cookies for 11 to 12 minutes, till their edges are chestnut brown and their tops are light golden brown, almost blonde. Remove them from the oven, and cool on the pan till they've set enough to move without breaking. Repeat with the remaining dough.

Use Resource 6 to practice measuring liquid volume.

II. Measuring the Volume of Regular Solids

Measuring solids is very different from measuring the volume of liquids. Liquids, you can pour! Solids, you can't. Our tools for measuring solids are familiar ones! Regular solids are things like boxes, bricks, books, and other solid items that are rectangular.

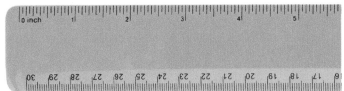

Measuring volume of regular solids is super easy. It is very much like measuring area (width x length). To measure volume, you just add one more measurement to the formula: width x length *x height*. More about measuring volume on the next page.

Right-brained tips for remembering the meaning of "volume."

Volume has three meanings:

1. A book which is one volume in a series.

2. How much space something takes up.

3. The loudness of sound.

"The volume (size) *of the volume* (book) *that crashed to the floor with loud volume* (sound) *- was big!"*

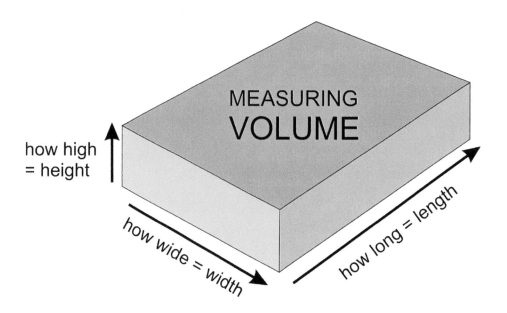

Look at the illustration above. Let's say this box has these measurements:

WIDTH: 8"

LENGTH: 11"

HEIGHT: 2"

The way to figure out the volume is to multiply 8 x 11 x 2: 8 x 11 = 88. 88 x 2 = 176. We can't just say the volume of the box is 176. Someone will definitely ask you, "inches or feet?" And we can't just say, "inches." We can't say, "square inches" like we did when we measured area. Because we are speaking of volume, we will say, "cubic inches." While a square is flat, a cube has height as well.

Here is the same box with the cubic inches marked. The area of the top of the box is 8 x 11 or 88 square inches. But the squares have height, so we call the top layer of the box 88 cubic inches. Then we add the second layer of cubic inches. 88 x 2 = 176 cubic inches.

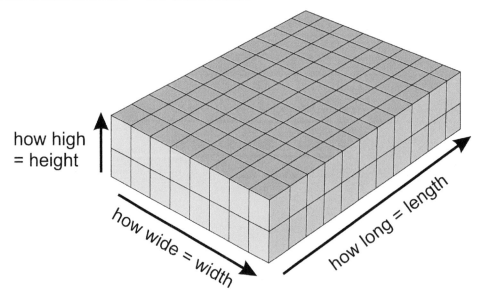

Practice Measuring Volume

Let's practice measuring volume. Find some items to measure - you could even use the same items you measured before in Chapter 3. In fact, to review measurement, let's do this:

1. Measure the *perimeter* of each item's top surface.

2. Measure the *area* of each item's top surface.

3. Measure the *mass/weight* of each item using a kitchen scale.

4. Measure the *volume* of each item.

When you have done these four things, you will know ALL about each of your items!

 Use Resource 6 to practice measuring volume of regular and irregular solids.

III. Measuring the Volume of Irregular Solids

This section is going to be so much fun! Measuring liquids and regular solids was kind of simple and not very exciting. What if you need to measure the volume of something that is very irregular? You can't pour it into a measuring cup, nor can you measure the sides.

Look at the dog on the right. How would you begin to measure the length, width, and height in order to find volume? You can't.

So, what you do is this:

Find a measuring cup that is a large enough to fit the dog inside of it. Set the dog inside the cup. Next, fill the cup with water, so that the water is above the dog's head and right at the top line on the cup. For example, if you use a 1 cup measuring cup, fill it with water so that the water touches the 1 cup line.

Now, take the dog out. Make a note of where the water is now. Say the top of the water in the cup is now at the ½ mark since you took the dog out. This means the volume of the dog is 4 ounces or ½ a cup.

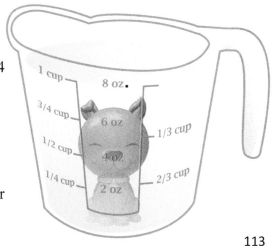

When you push an object into water, the object displaces, or moves aside, some water. The measurement lines on the cup show us just how much water was moved aside. How much water was pushed aside shows the volume of the object.

Part III
Measurement Resources

In the pages following are resources for you to use with your child to practice working with measurement. One sheet may or may not be enough practice. If you feel your child needs more practice, continue the measurement activities in a hands-on, real life way.

For example, R-1 "Practice with Tracking the Weather" can be repeated as many times as you would like. Just give your child a fresh copy of the sheet.

Tools needed for this section:

1. Outdoor thermometer, food thermometer, body thermometer
2. Ruler, yardstick, tape measure
3. Kitchen scales and bathroom scales
4. Measuring spoons and cups, pint, quart, and gallon containers

R-1 - Practice with Tracking the Weather

You will need a thermometer outside in a sheltered spot. Write the time of day and the temperature on the lines provided, then color in the mercury to match the temperature. The first one is done for you.

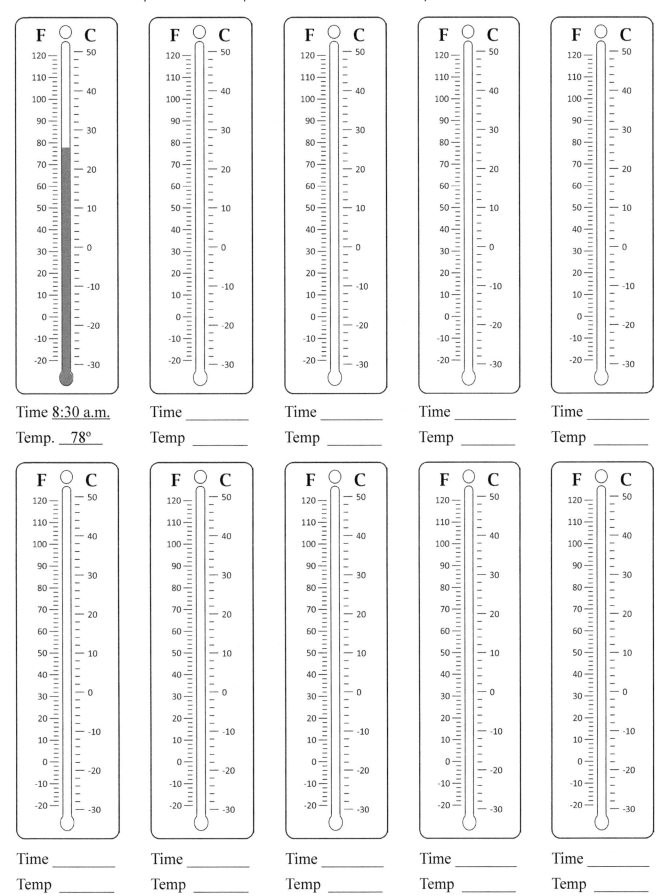

Time <u>8:30 a.m.</u>

Temp. <u>78°</u>

Time _____

Temp _____

Time _____

Temp _____

Time _____

Temp _____

Time _____

Temp _____

Time _____

Temp _____

Time _____

Temp _____

Time _____

Temp _____

Time _____

Temp _____

Time _____

Temp _____

R-1 - Practice Measuring the Temperature of Foods

Use a food thermometer and get help as needed as you measure the temperatures of various foods. For measuring temperature on a stove top, clip the thermometer to the inside of the pan so that the probe is in the food, but not touching the side of the pan. For baked foods, make sure the probe is in the meat, not touching a bone.

Applesauce

1. Cut up 3 pounds of apples.
2. Put in a saucepan and barely cover with water.
3. Add 2 teaspoons cinnamon
4. Clip thermometer to side of pan
5. Simmer until apples are soft
6. Push cooked apples through a ricer that will strain out the peels and seeds.

Record the temperature of the apples every 10 minutes.

Start temp: _____

10 minutes: _____

20 minutes: _____

30 minutes: _____

40 minutes: _____

Ricer

This activity uses the thermometer to record changing temperatures as a recipe cooks.

Baked Whole Chicken

1. Preheat oven to 350°.
2. Cover a baking sheet with foil.
3. Wash the chicken and pat it dry.
4. Mix 2 tablespoons soft butter with fresh, chopped herbs. Choose from rosemary, sage, thyme, parsley.
5. Rub the outside of the chicken with the butter/herb mixture.
6. Insert the thermometer into the leg, not touching the bone and bake until it reaches at least 165°.

Let the baked chicken rest for 30 minutes before cutting.

This activity uses the thermometer to make sure the chicken is fully cooked.

Yummy Corn Chowder

1. Peel and cut up 4 potatoes and chop 1 onion.
2. Open a can of creamed corn and put into a saucepan.
3. Add potatoes and onions to corn.
4. Add 2 cups chicken broth and salt and pepper to taste. Simmer for 20 minutes.
5. Clip thermometer to side of pan.
6. Add 2 cups warmed half & half just before time is up.

Record temperature of soup every 10 minutes.

10 minutes: _____

20 minutes: _____

30 minutes: _____

40 minutes: _____

This activity uses the thermometer to record changing temperatures as a recipe cooks.

Tangy, No-Fail Baked Chicken

1. Preheat oven to 350°.
2. Mix 1 cup catsup with ½ cup honey and ½ cup mustard.
3. Grease a long baking dish with butter or olive oil.
4. Spread chicken pieces even in pan and pour the sauce over it.
5. Insert the thermometer into a boneless piece of chicken.
6. Bake until the thermometer is at 165° (you can also use a slow cooker for this)

Half way through, spoon sauce over chicken. Serve over rice.

This activity uses the thermometer to make sure the chicken is fully cooked.

R-1 - Practice Measuring Body Temperature

Using a body thermometer, select several people and take their temperatures. Write down who they are and what their temperatures are. Next, draw a red line on the thermometers below them to show their temperatures.

1.

2.

3.

Name _____

Name _____

Name _____

Temp. _____

Temp. _____

Temp. _____

R-2 - Practice Measuring Length in Inches

Using a 12" ruler, measure the hands and feet where the red arrows show you to measure. Write down the measurement for each. In the top row, measure your own hand. In the second row, measure an adult's hand. In the third row, measure your foot and two other people's feet.

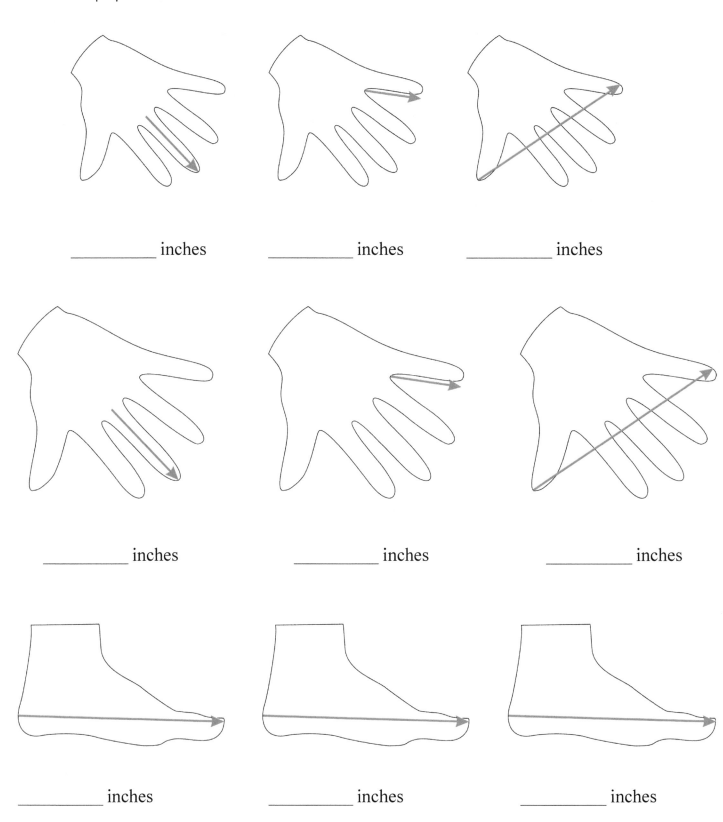

_____ inches   _____ inches   _____ inches

_____ inches   _____ inches   _____ inches

_____ inches   _____ inches   _____ inches

R-2 - Practice Measuring Length in Feet

Using a yardstick or tape measure, find the objects below - OR substitute other objects you find around you and measure them. Write the measurements of the longest side using the words "feet high, feet wide, or feet long." The first one is done for you.

4' tall

R-2 - Practice Measuring Length in Yards

Using a yardstick or tape measure, find the objects below - OR substitute other objects you find around you and measure the longest side. Write the measurements using the words "yards high, yards wide, aor yards long." The first one is done for you.

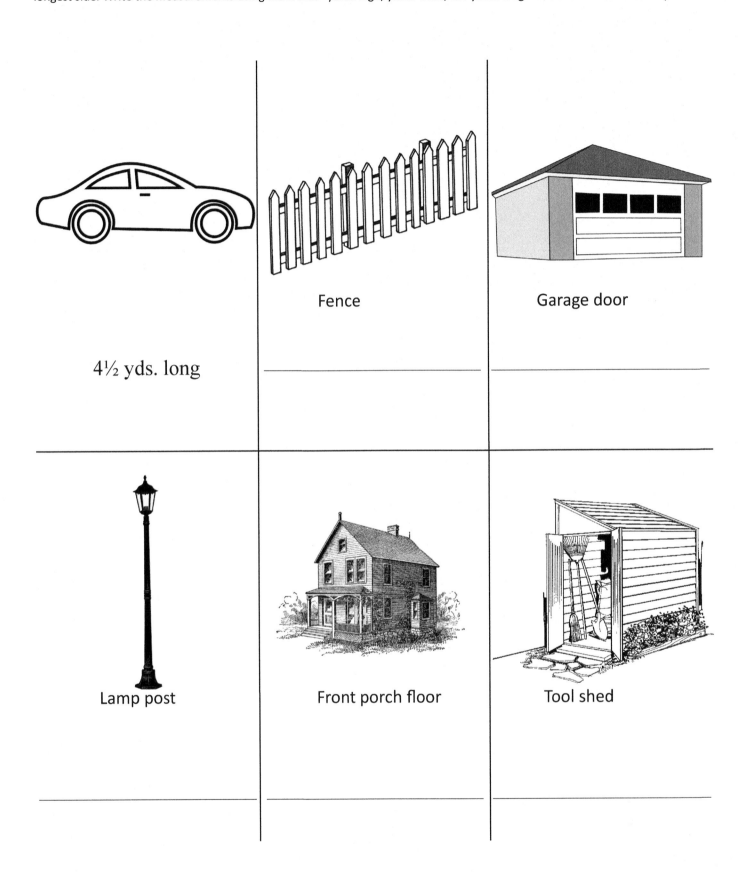

4½ yds. long

Fence

Garage door

Lamp post

Front porch floor

Tool shed

R-3 - Practice Measuring Perimeter in Inches

Using a 12" ruler, measure the perimeter of the top surface of each of these objects - or find some objects of your own that you would like to measure. Your answers will be in inches: "The perimeter of this potholder is 24"."

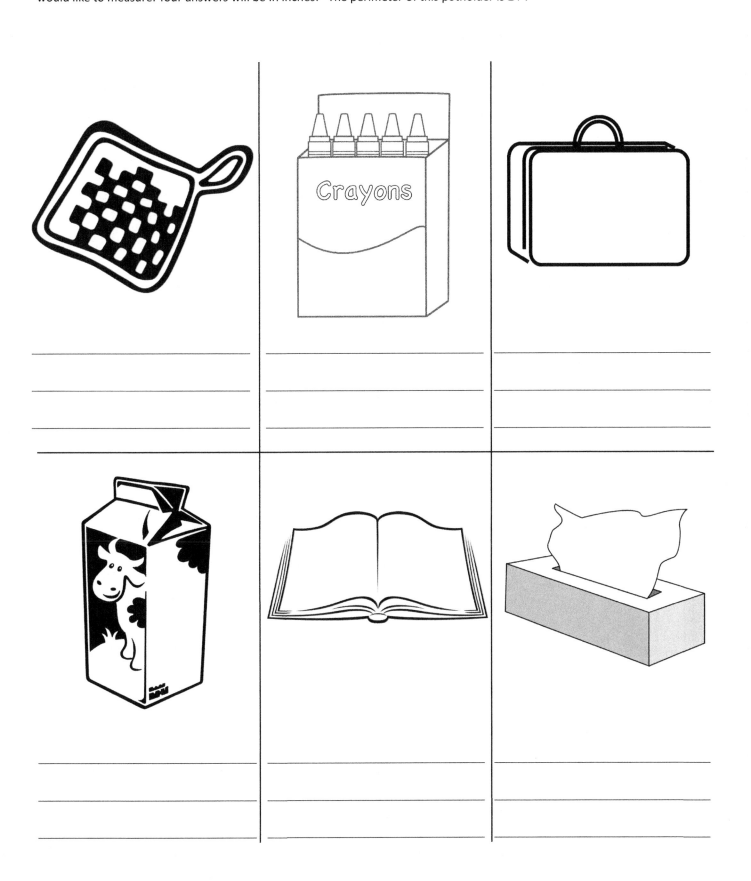

R-3 - Practice Measuring Perimeter in Feet

Using a tape measure, measure the perimeter of one of the surfaces of each of these objects - or find some objects of your own that you would like to measure. Your answers will be in feet: "The perimeter of this rug is 16 '." Remember that to find perimeter, you can add the length of all four sides, or you can add two sides (short side and long side) and mulitply by 2.

R-4 - Practice Measuring Area

Using a tape measure, measure the area of one of the surfaces of each of these objects - or find some objects of your own that you would like to measure. Your answers will be in square inches or square feet: "The area of this rug is 15 square feet." For any object that you don't have nearby, make up a size you think sounds good. You will need two sides. Calculate the area.

tabletop

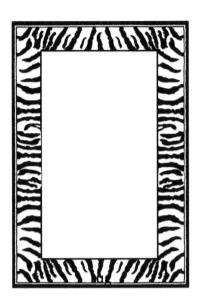

book cover

_____

_____

_____

garden

doghouse roof

treehouse floor

_____

_____

_____

R-5 - Practice Measuring Ounces & Pounds

Find 6 small objects around the house or classroom to weigh. You will need a kitchen scale, or a scale that weighs ounces and pounds. In each box write what you are weighing, or draw a picture of what you are weighing. Next, weigh each object and write how many ounces or pounds each object is.

R-5 - Practice Weighing People

Find 6 friends or family members who will allow you to weigh them using a bathroom scale. Record names and weights below.
Your answers will be written like this: "Tommy. 65 lbs."

1.

Name _____

Weight _____

2.

Name _____

Weight _____

3.

Name _____

Weight _____

4.

Name _____

Weight _____

5.

Name _____

Weight _____

6.

Name _____

Weight _____

R-6 - Practice Comparing Volume

Choose three containers that are different sizes. For example, you can use a shoebox, a paper cup, a large plastic tumbler, and a cereal bowl. You will also need a scale to weigh your items.

Shoebox Experiment

Fill the shoebox with T-shirts or pajamas. Weigh the box and write the weight here:

_____

Now, fill the shoebox with books. Weigh the shoebox again.

_____

Circle the weight that is heavier.

Paper Cup Experiment

Fill the paper cup with water. Weigh the cup of water and write the weight here:

_____

Now, fill the shoebox with sand or pebbles. Weigh the cup again.

_____

Circle the weight that is heavier.

Tumbler Experiment

Fill the tumbler with ice. Weigh the tumbler and write the weight here:

_____

Now, fill the tumbler with water. Weigh the tumbler again.

_____

Circle the weight that is lighter.

Cereal Bowl Experiment

Fill the cereal bowl with cereal. Weigh the bowl of cereal and write the weight here:

_____

Now, fill the cereal bowl with silverware. Weigh the cereal bowl again.

_____

Circle the weight that is lighter.

R-6 - Practice Measuring Liquid Volume

You will need measuring spoons and a measuring cup that shows 1 or 2 cups plus ounces. You will also need a pint jar, a quart jar, and an empty gallon jub. Work at the sink as you answer each question below.

Tablespoons to Ounces

Find the tablespoon measure. Locate 2 ounces on the measuring cup.

Fill your tablespoon to the brim with water and empty it into the measuring cup.

How many tablespoons does it take to make 2 ounces?

_____ tablespoons.

Cups to Pints

Fill the pint jar with water.

Now carefully fill your 1 cup measure with water from the pint jar.

Dump the water out and refill the cup.

How many cups are in a pint?

_____ cups.

Making a Gallon

Practice filling a gallon jug with your other measuring containers. Write down how many of each measuring container it took to fill a gallon.

_____ cups _____ pints _____ quarts

Ounces to Cups

Fill your measuring cup with water to the 4 ounce mark.

What part of a cup is 4 ounces?

_____cup

Now add water to the 6 ounce mark.

What part of a cup is 6 ounces?

_____cup

Cups and Pints to Quarts

Fill your measuring cup with water as you work to fill a quart jar with water.

How many cups did it take to fill a quart?

_____ cups.

Do the same thing with the pint jar.

How many pints make a quart?

_____pints.

R-6 - Practice Measuring Volume of Regular Solids

You will need some objects and some measuring tools: rulers, yardstick, and possibly a tape measure. Your answers will be in cubic inches or cubic feet depending on the size of the items you measure. You may measure the items below, or you can find your own. If you choose your own items, please write down what you measured and the volume for each.

Answer Key

In the pages following are answer keys. Several of the exercises don't have answer keys because the content of the activity is left up to the student.

TIME

p. 40, R-1
Col 1: 08:00, 11:00, 7:00, 4:00
Col. 2: Check to see if hand points to hour shown on digital clock.

p. 41, R-1.2
Answers will vary.

p. 42, R-2
Minute hands will all be on 12, and hour hands will match times on digital clocks.

p. 43, R-4.1
Minute hands will match the minutes shown on digital clocks.

p. 44, R-4.2
In rows 1 and 3, hands will point to places on the clocks matching times in the digital clocks.
Row 2: 07:08:16, 03:32:06, 10:22:46.

p.45, R-6.1
Row 1: 01:40, 06:50, 02:10
Row 2: 03:50, 03:20, 04:10
Row 3: 12:40, 08:45, 01:15

p. 46, R-6.2
Row 1: 01:25, 06:35, 01:55
Row 2: 03:35, 03:05, 03:55
Row 3: 12:25, 08:30, 01:00

p. 47, R-7
Row 1: Minute hands on 10, 7, 11
Row 2: Minute hands on 8, 9, 9
Row 3: Minute hands on 11, 10, 8

p.48, R-8
Row 1: Minute hand on 11, 4, 9
Row 2: Minute hand on 11, 1, 3
Row 3: Minute hand on 10, 8, 11

p. 49, R-9.1 (minute hand/end time)
Row 1: 12/02:00, 4/06:20, 5/03:25
Row 2: 7/02:35, 5/04:25, 3/03:15
Row 3: 4/01:20, 7/08:35, 1/11:05

p. 50, R-9.2 (Minute, Hour)
Row 1: M:12, H:3; M:4, H:past 7; M:5, H:past 4
Row 2: M:7, H:past 3; M:5, H: past 5; M:3, H:4
Row 3: M:4, H:past 2; M:7, H:past 9; M:1, H:11

p. 51, R-10
Row 1: M:7, 6:35; M:9, 1:45; M:8, 3:40
Row 2: M:3, 5:15; M:6, 1:30; M:11, 7:55

p.52, R-11
Answers will vary

MONEY
p. 81, R-1
Answers will vary

p.82, R-2
Row 1:
11 nickels
13 nickels, 3 pennies
Row 2:
15 nickels, 2 pennies
4 nickels, 2 pennies
Row 3:
11 nickels, 3 pennies
11 nickels, 4 pennies
Row 4:
3 nickels
15 nickels, 4 pennies

p.83, R-3
Row 1:
4 dimes, 1 nickel, 4 pennies
8 dimes, 2 pennies
Row 2:
3 dimes, 1 nickel, 2 pennies
5 dimes, 1 nickel, 4 pennies
Row 3:
5 dimes, 1 nickel, 3 pennies
6 dimes, 1 nickel, 2 pennies
Row 4:
8 dimes, 1 nickel, 1 penny
2 dimes, 1 nickel, 3 pennies

p. 84, R-4 (options)
Row 1:
2 quarters, 1 nickel, 4 pennies
3 quarters, 2 dimes, 4 pennies
Row 2:
3 quarters, 2 pennies
2 quarter, 3 pennies
Row 3:
1 quarter, 2 dimes, 3 pennies
2 quarters, 1 nickel, 2 pennies
Row 4:
2 quarters, 1 dime, 1 nickel, 1 penny
3 quarters, 1 dime, 3 pennies

p. 85, R-5
Row 1:
1 dollar, 1 quarter, 1 dime, 4 pennies
2 dollars, 2 quarters, 1 dime, 1 nickel, 4 pennies
Row 2:
1 dollar, 1 dime, 1 nickel, 4 pennies
3 dollars, 3 quarters, 1 dime, 4 pennies
Row 3:
2 dollars, 2 quarters, 1 penny
1 dollar, 3 quarters, 1 dime, 4 pennies
Row 4:
1 dollar, 1 dime
2 dollars, 2 quarters, 1 dime, 1 nickel, 3 pennies

p. 86, R-6
Row 1:
1 $10.00, 1 $1.00, 1 quarter, 1 dime, 1 penny
1 $10.00, 2 $1.00, 2 quarters, 1 nickel, 3 pennies
Row 2:
1 $10.00, 1 quarter, 4 pennies
1 $10.00, 1 $5.00, 2 $1.00, 1 quarter, 2 dimes, 4 pennies
Row 3:
1 $10.00, 1 $5.00, 2 quarters, 1 nickel, 2 pennies
1 $5.00, 3 $1.00, 1 quarter, 4 pennies
Row 4:
1 $10.00, 3 $1.00, 3 quarters, 2 dimes, 2 pennies
1 $5.00, 1 $1.00, 3 quarters, 4 pennies

p. 87, R-7
Answers will vary. Example answer = $6.78

p. 88, R-8
Row 1:
$10.00/4 pennies, 1 dime, 2 quarters
Row 2:
$20.00/1 penny, 2 dimes, 2 quarters
Row 3:
$20.00/3 pennies, 1 quarter, 1 nickel, 1 dime
Row 4:
$10.00/3 pennies

p. 89, R-8
Row 1:
$20.00/1 nickel, 1 $5.00
Row 2:
$20.00/1 penny, 1 nickel, 1 dime, 3 quarters, 2 $1.00
Row 3:
$10.00/1 penny, 1 nickel, 1 quarter
Row 4:
$10.00/4 pennies, 2 quarters, 2 $1.00

MEASUREMENT
p. 115, R-1
Answers will vary

p.116. R-1
Answers will vary

p. 117, R-1
Answers will vary

p. 118, R-2
Answers will vary

p. 119, R-2
Children will choose the longest side and use that as length, but answers will be so many feet tall or so many feet long.

p. 120, R-2
Children will choose the longest side and use that as length, but answers will be so many yards tall or so many yards long.

p. 121, R-3
Answers will vary.

p. 122, R-3
Answers will vary.

p. 123, R-4
Answers will vary.

p. 124, R-5
Answers will vary.

p. 125, R-5
Answers will vary.

p. 126, R-6
Answers will vary.

p. 127, R-6
Row 1:
4 tablespoons, 1/2 cup, 3/4 cup
Row 2:
2 cups, 4 cups, 2 pints
Row 3:
16 cups, 8 pints, 4 cups

p. 128, R-6
Answers will vary

CPSIA information can be obtained
at www.ICGtesting.com
Printed in the USA
LVOW05s1752280218
568139LV00008B/13/P